D0143140

HARD-EARNED
LESSONS FROM
COUNSELLING

IN *Action*

**COUNSELLING
· IN ACTION ·**

Series editor: Windy Dryden

Counselling in Action is a series of books developed especially for counsellors and students of counselling which provides clear and explicit guidelines for counselling practice. A special feature of the series is the emphasis it places on the *process* of counselling.

Titles include:

Feminist Counselling in Action
Jocelyn Chaplin

Gestalt Counselling in Action
Petrüska Clarkson

Integrative Counselling Skills in Action
Sue Culley

Key Issues for Counselling in Action
Edited by Windy Dryden

Training and Supervision for Counselling in Action
Edited by Windy Dryden and Brian Thorne

Personal Construct Counselling in Action
Fay Fransella and Peggy Dalton

Psychodynamic Counselling in Action
Michael Jacobs

Experiences of Counselling in Action
Edited by Dave Mearns and Windy Dryden

Person-Centred Counselling in Action
Dave Mearns and Brian Thorne

Transactional Analysis Counselling in Action
Ian Stewart

Cognitive-Behavioural Counselling in Action
Peter Trower, Andrew Casey and Windy Dryden

HARD-EARNED
LESSONS FROM
COUNSELLING

EDITED BY
WINDY DRYDEN

SAGE Publications
London • Newbury Park • New Delhi

© Preface, Chapter 4 and editorial arrangement © Windy
Dryden, 1992
Chapter 1 © Petrūska Clarkson, 1992
Chapter 2 © Peggy Dalton, 1992
Chapter 3 © Emmy van Deurzen-Smith, 1992
Chapter 5 © Michael Jacobs, 1992
Chapter 6 © Dave Mearns, 1992
Chapter 7 © Pat Milner, 1992
Chapter 8 © John Rowan, 1992
Chapter 9 © Robin Shohet, 1992
Chapter 10 © Moira Walker, 1992

First published 1992

All rights reserved. No part of this publication may be
reproduced, stored in a retrieval system, transmitted or
utilized in any form or by any means, electronic,
mechanical, photocopying, recording or otherwise, without
permission in writing from the Publishers.

SAGE Publications Ltd
6 Bonhill Street
London EC2A 4PU

SAGE Publications Inc
2455 Teller Road
Newbury Park, California 91320

SAGE Publications India Pvt Ltd
32, M-Block Market
Greater Kailash – I
New Delhi 110 048

British Library Cataloguing in Publication Data

Hard-Earned Lessons from Counselling in Action. –
(Counselling in Action Series)
  I. Dryden, Windy II. Series
  361.3

  ISBN 0–8039–8668–8
  ISBN 0–8039–8669–6 (pbk)

Library of Congress catalog card number 92–056708

Typeset by Mayhew Typesetting, Rhayader, Powys
Printed in Great Britain by Hartnolls Ltd, Bodmin,
Cornwall

FLORIDA GULF COAST
UNIVERSITY LIBRARY

Contents

Preface

The purpose of this book is to show that *all* counsellors, no matter how experienced, have had to, and may well continue to have to, learn painful, hard-earned lessons about the counselling process. Having well-known practitioners share such experiences and the lessons that were learned has, I believe, underscored this point.

I asked the contributors to write a chapter on five hard-earned lessons they have learned over the course of their careers as practitioners of counselling. A 'hard-earned lesson' is here defined broadly as *something learned about the practice of counselling the hard way*.

The contributors were asked to write each lesson in a way that communicates the lesson they learned and the circumstances that preceded it. In particular, they were to focus on any issues they neglected before 'learning their lesson'. Brief examples, at least one per 'lesson', were required in order to solidify their learning. Contributors were also asked to identify any themes that emerged from the five pieces in their concluding comments. So clearly have they done this, that any final chapter which attempted to summarize the themes would have been repetitive and thus redundant. Consequently, I have let the contributors speak for themselves. In doing so I recognize that the 'lessons' they discuss are not exhaustive, but rather representative of all that the counselling process can throw up.

It is my particular hope that this volume gives comfort to trainee and beginning counsellors, who often struggle in their work with clients, falsely convinced that experienced practitioners have not encountered similar struggles. If nothing else, the chapters in this book give lie to this myth.

Windy Dryden

1 Petrūska Clarkson

When I was seven years old, I decided to become a 'brain surgeon' so I could be a doctor of unhappy minds and 'make them better'. Several career decisions later, I started formal training and learning to be a clinical psychologist, a counsellor, and then a psychotherapist. I had the deep and abiding hope that I could find understanding of the sadness and distress of human pain, learn the skills of helping people to free themselves from the shackles of their conditioning, their restricted beliefs and cultural limitations, and develop the necessary personal qualities which would transform my promising potential for healing into the genuine article.

I studied Carl Rogers; I went on encounter groups; I did a Freudian analysis with a Tavistock-trained analyst; I learnt about changing organizational systems from American university teachers; I worked in suicide prevention and in mental hospitals, advertising, and universities; I had a brief and unhappy excursion with a Kleinian analyst; I experienced and trained in gestalt, transactional analysis, bioenergetics, individual psychoanalysis, group psychotherapy, family therapy, sex therapy, suicide prevention and crisis counselling. These were not light studies. I gave several of these systems many years – an unstinting fortune in very hard-earned money, time, and energy. I had a quest.

I studied and studied, racing from degree to degree. I eventually admitted to myself that my thesis was an attempt to 'find the truth' about human haziness and unhappiness. I continued to hope that the real truth, the genuine key, was in the next book, in the next lecture I would attend, or the next experiential understanding carved from my own personal struggles with my inner demons. I loved, I married, eventually I created a family. I found a guru, said my mantra and meditated on the Buddha nature for many years. The need of the world was so great. Somewhere, surely, people really knew how to help people efficiently, truly, and without taking years and fortunes to do it. I travelled Europe and North America in search of teachers. I studied at the Tavistock, the Institute of Group Analysis; I spent eight more years in Jungian analysis. One conference I attended included 7,000 psychotherapists. If the truth was not there, where could it possibly be?

The strength of my dedication and commitment was impeccable; but I was still not finding the truth about making people better, the right way – the guaranteed, successful theory and method of treating people. If only I was more intelligent, could read faster, and learn better! Perhaps it was only my ignorance, laziness, or personal weakness which prevented me from discovering where and how?

While this is a description of my existential condition before I learned the major lesson, of which five examples follow, the issue of the healing factor was embedded in my search. It was present and I knew about it, yet never before was it as vivid and obvious. It is difficult for a fish to study and discuss water, since it is the very medium of its life. It is also difficult for psychotherapists and counsellors to study the *relationship*, since that is the very 'water' in which we and our clients live and breathe and find our meaning. I studied and honed and experienced and interpreted and used 'the relationship'. I thought it was the context for the rest of the work. I did not fully realize that it was *the work itself*. I do not believe I have ever seen it as clearly as I see it now. This does not mean I did not see it then; only that the figure and ground has shifted irrevocably, and I cannot overvalue its importance now.

There is also circumstantial validation, and evidence from the world of psychotherapy is amplifying the lesson. It is one of the most important factors in the rise of integrative psychotherapy (Norcross, 1986). For decades there have been attempts to find which psychotherapy, which counselling method was the more effective; which theory better, which approach more efficient in terms of money, time, and benefits (whether physical or spiritual). Now the bulk of research points to the fact that the most important factor is *the relationship* between the client and the counsellor.

When I look back on all the varieties of transformative or healing experiences in which I took part, it is the relationship between me and my psychotherapist that was the most important, vastly the most important. The theory they espoused, the interventions or interpretations they used, all these seem as nothing compared with the vitality of a rich network of relational possibilities, well orchestrated by a healing and committed significant 'other'. The most significant psychotherapist of my life said to me some three years ago, when she broke (again) one of the many technical prohibitions of the system of which she is a doyenne, 'We don't do rules around here – we're experienced enough to know they don't work! The rules, the guidelines – they are good for the beginners.' Rules can prevent harm, but taken as true in themselves, they can prevent healing. Ever since the Fiedler (1950) studies, it has been one of the best-kept secrets in psychotherapy that the more experienced people resemble each other more than novices resemble their seniors in that theoretical (ideological?) system. This fits my experience. The task is not solely that of the counsellor or psychotherapist. The work lies in between, in the relationship. Much else is error.

I now understand that this is the field to study. The particular theory seems secondary to the understanding and the skilful use of self in relationship. I have identified five different kinds of psycho-therapeutic relationship which are potentially available for constructive use in psychotherapy (Clarkson, 1991). These are: the working alliance; the transferential/counter-transferential relation-ship; the reparative/developmentally needed relationship; the person-to-person relationship; and the transpersonal relationship.

The working alliance is the part of the client–psychotherapist relationship that enables the client and therapist to work together even when the client experiences strong desires to the contrary. The transferential/counter-transferential relationship is the experience of unconscious wishes and fears transferred into the therapeutic partnership. The reparative/developmentally needed relationship is the intentional provision by the psychotherapist of a corrective, reparative, or replenishing relationship or action where the original parenting was deficient, abusive, or over-protective. The person-to-person relationship is the real relationship or core relationship – the opposite of object relationship. The transpersonal relationship is the timeless facet of the psychotherapeutic relationship, which is impossible to describe, but refers to the spiritual dimension of the healing relationship. It is important to remember these are not *stages* but *states* in psychotherapy, often subtly 'overlapping', in and between which a client construes his or her unique experiences.

These five relationship modalities can act as an integrative framework for different traditions or approaches to psycho-therapy, notwithstanding apparently irreconcilable schisms. I do not offer it as a new truth, only as a useful way in which to keep questing. I believe I have made most of my errors in counselling when I have confused the types of relationship which would be appropriate in the counselling with a particular person, or at a particular stage in their counselling or psychotherapy. I hope others will use these, not as rules, but as lessons for themselves. I have made some mistakes and learnt from them. Even so, there is still much to learn.

You are never off duty until the client has left the office

The first hard-earned lesson I can think of is when I unwittingly used the transpersonal to undermine therapeutic work. The client

was intending going to a job interview the next day, and was assuming a rather fatalistic attitude about it. He believed it was all 'in the
stars', or at least in God's hands. He was not used to making decisions in an active way, having had a childhood in which decisions
were made for him; for example, his family had moved frequently
due to his father's alcoholism, with the result that he had gone to
fifteen schools. Each time the family moved, it came as a surprise
to him. The children were never consulted, or given adequate
preparation time to adjust to a new situation that was not of their
own choosing. As with many children of alcoholics, he had lost the
causal connection between his deeds and behaviours and their
effects on others in the environment.

We spent substantial time in psychotherapy exploring his
pervasive sense of being a victim of circumstance, who might receive
either gifts or blows without any apparent causal connection. On
previous occasions he had relived and emotionally expressed some
confusion, rage, and pain associated with his original powerless
position in the world. Gradually, he learned to take responsibility
for himself, but still fell back into magical thinking and superstition
when under stress, as, for example, with this job interview.

I spent most of the therapy exploring with him the futility and
denial of personal autonomy and responsibility involved in magical
thinking and superstition. It sounds less delicate in abbreviation,
but it would be fair to say that we used the session to discuss taking
responsibility for one's own actions; the satisfactions of an
autonomous life; the naïvety of believing that one can make
something happen or prevent it happening by thinking about it; the
origins of his powerless feelings from childhood. This was
contrasted with my client's childhood belief that if he wished
somebody dead, the hated person might actually drop dead.

In counselling and psychotherapy it is important to clarify to the
client that there is often a difference between fantasy and reality.
Furthermore, it is empowering for people to begin to assume
responsibility for much of what they thought was outside their
power to influence. This sense of increasing personal focusing is a
highly important value in my approach to counselling.

After a session rich in these explorations, I accompanied my
client to the door. As he left I gaily waved to him, 'Good luck!' I
could see his face reassuming the fatalistic stare with which he had
entered my consulting room. I believe there is a transpersonal
element in human life, but for this particular client at this particular
moment it was unhelpful to invoke it. I painfully realized I had
effectively demolished much of the work we had done in the
session.

There is growing evidence to the effect that 'extra-analytic occurrences' affect psychotherapy and counselling far more than has been allowed for. It is very clear to me that this was an example of 'going off duty' before the session was completed; that is, moving to a social type of interaction which can effectively destroy or undermine – or at the very least not reinforce or substantiate – the most important aspects of the counselling. A similar situation may arise with a counsellor who responds to the client who says his mother has died: 'I'm sorry to hear that; you must be very sad.' By using the stereotypical social response, the psychotherapist deprives the person of a permissive atmosphere in which to express, for example, not sadness but perhaps joy and relief, about which the person may feel very guilty but which is nonetheless a more authentic expression of his real feelings, which he may not easily express to anyone except a counsellor. In this case, although my response was due to a premature 'going off duty', an apparent social level response, I had evoked supernatural powers, thus crediting them, not my client, with the primary capacity to influence the outcome of the job interview.

Being the 'good parent' can backfire

Another hard-earned lesson was when I discovered that providing a developmentally needed relationship when the relationship was still in the transference/counter-transference vector can be counterproductive.

I had already worked with this particular client for some time, so I believed we had a good working alliance and that I could provide her with a beneficial reparative experience. She originally came complaining of low self-esteem, self-destructive behaviours such as wrist-cutting, and compulsive promiscuity. She came from a family background of severe physical and sexual abuse. She had grown up with virtually no encouragement or support for her developing personhood. She was used to constant criticism of herself, her behaviour, her dislikes, and her interests. Indeed, the poverty of her early experiences was palpable in her victim-like demeanour and in the defeated way in which she held her body.

She had become so used to negative attention that she could hardly recognize or respond to friendliness from co-workers, kindness from potential friends, or the psychotherapist's nonjudgemental acceptance. During her quite long period in psychotherapy, she projected on to me the critical, judgemental, even hostile, motivations of her parents. It was only gradually, as she learned to express her angry feelings and release some of the pain which she had stored in her body and her heart, that it became possible for her to be in the world without the certain anticipation of rejection and injury. Containing her rage, mirroring her distress, and empathically entering into this painful inner world seemed to form the major part of our psychotherapeutic work. After some time it began to seem that she had worked through her transferential need to experience me as a hostile or rejecting parent. She developed a desire to be recognized for her progress, and said she wanted some appreciation from me.

At this point, she said to me one day that she had for the first time since entering treatment invited a friend out for a meal. This was a breakthrough because until then she had lacked the self-confidence or the motivation to attempt what was for her such a brave venture. Believing that by now she deserved and could use some positive support, I made a comment to the effect that she had done very well. The next week she phoned to say she was too scared to come for a session. I wrote offering her her usual time the following week, encouraging her to contact me so that we could deal with whatever the problem was. When we eventually met, she hesitantly explained she had lost her trust in me when I showed my appreciation of her progress, because it seemed to her that I couldn't possibly mean it in a sincere way; I was just setting her up in order to reject her later, as she had experienced in the past.

This was a powerful and humbling lesson for me, since it reminded me how easy it is to misjudge the readiness of patients for the corrective emotional experience or reparative work. Even though my client was able to use my positive encouragement later, at this stage it was mistimed. I had given the matter of starting to offer positive experience a great deal of thought and supervision before implementing it, so I was shocked and surprised to understand the fragility of the working alliance and the strength of the transference.

Having studied and struggled with the intricacies of the developmentally needed relationship, this incident has served to increase my caution about providing potentially reparative experiences for clients without providing very clear mutual agreements. In situations where the transference dynamic may be actively or passively present, there is risk of undermining the adult–adult working alliance to an extent where a potentially beneficial intervention can perpetuate or reinforce negative life patterns (Balint, 1959).

We cannot live by analysis alone

Early in my career, when I was still very influenced and impressed by my orthodox psychoanalytic training, I persisted in working within the transference mode – at the expense of validating the personal humanity of the client with whom I was working. A particular client taught me about this.

The client was middle-aged, a mother of six demanding children, with a husband who vacillated between being demanding and cold. She held her body in a sunken position, as if she had symbolically been kicked. Even though her deprivation of affection and her yearning for comfort tugged at my heart, I solidly interpreted her need for touch and reassurance in line with my training and psychoanalytic supervision, that is, I consistently refused to answer personal questions or to accede to human requests, for a hand to be held or a warm word of reassurance to be spoken as such action had been construed as non-analytic. This 'abstinent' manner was the way I had been treated in my first psychoanalysis, and I was modelling this.

A colleague of mine has said that most people are so badly treated in their homes of origin in childhood they will tolerate a remarkable level of deprivation in psychotherapy or counselling because it is not as bad as what originally happened to them. At least I was present for this client and did not abuse her, but I was analyzing her transference towards me.

After too long a time, my confidence in my therapeutic abilities grew, and competence in understanding and utilizing my own counter-transference issues developed sufficiently for me to respond spontaneously to her. The day she held out her hand again to me in a very tentative, supplicating way, and I reached out to hold it in a simple, human, compassionate way, I truly learnt the value of person-to-person relationship and the futility of applying prescriptions or proscriptions to the human spirit. She knew what she needed to be healed, which was subsequently borne out by her therapeutic progress – a human touch. I was moved by her and by her pain, and touched by her experience to feel an empathy that could only flower in human mutuality.

Throughout the last twenty years of studying this field (and for most of this time I have been in psychoanalysis or psychotherapy of some kind), I have moved further and further away from appreciating the relevance of withholding person-to-person acknowledgement, and have become more profoundly impressed, touched, and awed by the healing capacity of a skilled clinician working within the person-to-person relationship. In addition to my personal experience, I have watched some of my colleagues in protracted psychoanalysis become more depersonalized as they attempt to model themselves on the depersonalizing analytic relationship, whereas they went into psychoanalysis seeking how to be more intimate with others. Distortion probably creates distortion, as the subtle induction for the patient to display resistance probably creates resistance. Woodmansey (1988) recently challenged the psychoanalytic establishment: 'Perhaps we are doing our patients harm when we do not touch them?' Certainly it is possible that 'good' is thus not being done.

I have taken very seriously research which shows that positive or negative expectations in educational situations can significantly affect the performance of students. There is research evidence that school children and students respond differentially to their teachers' unvoiced expectations of them (Rosenthal and Jacobson, 1968). When teachers believed children were unintelligent and could not learn, the children responded with lowered performance, no matter what their original gifts. Positive expectations influenced the students' performance in positive ways. There may be a lesson for psychotherapists: expect resistance and investment in the *status quo*, and those phenomena are more likely to recur. Perhaps our expectations of our clients to grow positively and be willing to take responsibility may enhance the likelihood that they will manifest these qualities in counselling and in life (Clarkson, 1989). Perhaps when we add the person-to-person relationship to that of the trans-ference/counter-transference relationships at the appropriate time in an individual's therapy, the ultimate work of transformation can be enhanced. As Jung (1928) said, 'Learn your theories as well as you can, but put them aside when you touch the miracle of the living soul. Not theories but your own creative individuality alone must decide.'

'Being strong' can be bad modelling

Sensitive people are alive to their surroundings. They therefore pick up on unspoken personal anguish or stress in those around them, including (especially?) their psychotherapists. They know something is wrong, and if no explanation is given, they may experience a strong need to heal the psychotherapist (Searles, 1975). Alternatively, they may fantasize their own explanation for the psychotherapist's distress. In any case, such fantasies, projec-tions, or unvoiced fears may undermine the fabric of the working alliance in psychotherapy, which needs to be strong enough to be effective, in order to sustain the heights and the depths of transferential and other concerns which people bring.

Typical fantasized explanations include, 'She's ill'. 'She's angry with me'. 'I'm too much for her'. 'She's not well enough to look after me', and so on. If this is part of the client's script, he or she may then protect or nurture the psychotherapist, possibly skirting around issues perceived, rightly or wrongly, as draining or distressing to the therapist, such as the expression of rage or hatred. This suppression then naturally hinders or prolongs the healing course of psychotherapy, and may reinforce the patient's damaging or limiting script. This process is frequently dealt with by clients who, with a second or third psychotherapist begin to talk about issues they could not share with the first. For example, the psychoanalyst Alice Miller had completed a psychoanalysis without uncovering her own early childhood abuse.

One of the great many ways of keeping the working alliance intact is to clear out of the way realistic factors impinging upon it, as in this example of not acknowledging things that are true, at the same time as using fears and fantasies to explore and understand the irrational and unconscious motivations at work in human life. As a result, I think I have erred on the side of being overly cautious on occasion. For example, on one occasion I came into a group psychotherapy session feeling tired. Intending to maintain scrupulous boundaries and not to make an inappropriate self-disclosure, I did not say that I had been up all night sitting with a sick friend. The group members were rather subdued, until towards the end of the session when one member risked saying, 'You seem very tense today.' The others joined in, sharing that they had imagined I was cross or ill. I realized then that it was important to explain to them that I was indeed tired, and why, and to reassure them that this was nothing they had done, nor was it something I was not aware of or could not cope with.

This experience demonstrated to me the importance of appropriate self-disclosure when there are relevant current stresses or current events in the psychotherapist's life which may impinge upon or disturb their habitual range of emotional responsiveness. The art lies in the subtlety of perceiving what is appropriate. The psychotherapist must decide whether to withhold or to give sufficient information in order for the two parties to have an authentic relationship. The opportunity for self-disclosure is clearly not to be interpreted as an invitation to speak at length about issues of personal concern.

In this context, it is also important for psychotherapists to distinguish clearly between the occasions when they are capable of working competently even though tired or stressed, and when they are not competent to work. For example, after a major bereavement, I cancelled all my work for two weeks. When I started seeing clients again, I acknowledged I was still grieving, and yet I was still able to work. At the beginning of one session, I saw my client watching me intently. I said, 'I think you think I've been crying.' She nodded. I confirmed, 'Yes, I have been crying, but I feel much better now, and am ready to work with you.'

Who? Me?

As psychotherapists, we are often fully trained and willing to deal with negative transference in its many forms: rejection, criticism, erotic transference, over-idealization, distrust, disappointment, being ignored, or even hostile attacks. For many psychotherapists, dealing with negative transferences is more comfortable than dealing with positive transferences.

It is often more comfortable for a psychotherapist, particularly of existential persuasions, to encourage clients to assume egalitarian and mutual positions. A concern for the client's empowerment and a desire for them to re-own their positive projections can easily lead to the psychotherapist avoiding, rejecting, or preventing the client's genuine needs to love and admire the psychotherapist. It is essential for this kind of positive feeling to be received, heard, and valued. This reluctance to accept the client's self-object need to love and admire the psychotherapist can be debilitating in the long run if, in fact, it is therapeutically indicated (Kohut, 1977).

In the past I would not fully receive clients' love, believing they were projecting an idealizing transference on to me. I have learnt over the years from these same clients that they felt rejected when they felt their love was not received and accepted; some felt diminished – maybe their love was not even worth having. They got the emotional message, 'I don't care whether or not you love me', or the intellectual message, 'No, you don't love me – it's just positive transference or idealization.' Whatever their particular interpretation was, the client dismissed their intrinsic feelings, and a move towards creativity, spontaneity, openness and love was laid aside.

From the authenticity of the joy with which people have told me they loved me, I have in more recent years learned just how important, genuine, and unfulfilled is the need to love. One client taught me this in particular. From when she was an infant, Trudy was abused by a cruel and envious mother. They were temperamentally mismatched and did not like each other as people. The mother resented her daughter even for being born at all, even though one imagines that a baby comes into the world wishing to love and be loved. This was barren ground indeed for the flowering of any such mutual fondness. After many years of therapy, working through rage, abandonment, distress, neglect, and release from the self-disgust which Trudy had incorporated and introjected from her mother, she appeared to re-connect with a healthy, human desire to give her love. One day Trudy wrote me a letter telling me how much she loved me:

> It is more important for me to feel and express love than to experience it, and important to let myself feel such a positive feeling towards an older woman. I feel more whole and healthy as a person and as a woman, in finding that I can experience and express affection, and for this to be received.

From my own life, and experience in psychotherapy as the client, I have also learned this – that my gift of healing needs to be accepted and valued, and that my need to love is greater than my need to be loved. The primary need of human beings is to love – in Fairbairn's (1952) terms, human beings are 'object seeking'. This instinctive need to love can often be a profoundly unmet need. Psychotherapists sometimes have genuine difficulties in accepting and validating this kind of pure, untrammelled love. It is, however, frequently a feature of a healed soul, in gratitude for gifts given and gifts received, in mutual recognition of a shared humanity.

Conclusion

These are moments from the mass of complexity and paradox which constitutes psychotherapy, offered as fragmented reflections of my own learning. Whatever value readers may get from them is more to do with what it makes them think, and what it sparks off in them than with what I can encapsulate in these brief segments.

I have learnt how important it is to the process of psychotherapy to be aware which kind of relationship I am engaging in with a person, which kind is needed, and which could be potentially unproductive and dangerous. Determining this is made more complex by the fact that a client's relationship needs or 'danger areas' may change from second to second. One way of conceptualizing the psychotherapeutic relationship is as the psychotherapist voluntarily entering into a kinship relationship with the client. Relationship is the first condition of being human, and it creates a bond between two individuals that is far more than the sum of its parts. I have also learned that it is important to stay in psychotherapy for myself, and to be well supported by frequent supervision.

If we are to grow and not merely to change, then our entire lives are a lesson; presented not as a neat series of graded steps, but often as a bewildering range of choices and implications. Very often a lesson will be re-presented to us many times over in different guises until we finally learn its meaning. When consciously entering any obvious phase of learning, such as embarking on a course of psychotherapy training, one sees the opportunity to learn as a pleasant experience, and so it very often is – but at times we are reminded abruptly that learning can seem painful as well as supportive. Learning in life is a creative endeavour, and, like all creative endeavours, exists in itself, as itself, to infinity. As with expressions of creativity, the learning process can be perceived as good, bad, or indifferent – it is the perception of the personal truths embedded within it that is life-enhancing.

References

Balint, M. (1959) *Thrills and Regressions*. London: Hogarth Press.

Clarkson, P. (1989) *Gestalt Counselling in Action*. London: Sage.

Clarkson, P. (1991) 'A multiplicity of psychotherapeutic relationships', *British J. Psychotherapy*, 7(2): 148–63.

Fairbairn, W. R. D. (1952) *Psycho-Analytic Studies of the Personality*. London: Tavistock.

Fiedler, F. E. (1950) 'A comparison of therapeutic relationships, in psychoanalytic, non-directive and Adlerian therapy', *J. Consulting Psychology*, 14: 436–45.

Jung, C. G. (1928) 'Analytical psychology and education', in H. G. and C. F. Baynes (trans.), *Contributions to Analytical Psychology*. London and New York: Trench Trubner.

Kohut, H. (1977) *The Restoration of the Self*. New York: International Universities Press.

Norcross, J. C. (ed.) (1986) *Handbook of Eclectic Psychotherapy*. New York: Brunner/Mazel.

Rosenthal, R. and Jacobson, L. (1968) *Pygmalion in the Classroom: Teachers' Expectations and Pupils' Intellectual Development*. New York: Holt, Reinhart and Winston.

Searles, H. F. (1975) 'The patient as therapist to his analyst', in P. L. Giovacchini (ed.), *Tactics and Techniques in Psychoanalytic Therapy*, Vol. II (94–151). New York: Aronson.

Woodmansey, A. C. (1988) 'Are psychotherapists out of touch?', *British J. Psychotherapy*, 5(1): 57–65.

2 Peggy Dalton

My basic training was in speech therapy. For some years I worked with a varied caseload, then came to specialize in work with children and adults who stuttered. My training had equipped me to assess and 'treat' the problems; it had in no way prepared me to understand the people with those problems, or to take account of their view of their worlds, themselves, or what was going wrong for them. That was a long time ago, and I am assured that things have improved, that there is greater focus on the person as a whole and the circumstances in which they have to lead their lives.

Many speech therapists have always taken time to listen to clients and their families, and the realization that people rather than programmes will govern the success of any form of remediation has grown. Nevertheless, many of us have become dissatisfied over the years with our lack of skill in addressing the psychological complexities presented by people with speech, language, and voice problems, which can seriously constrict their lives. Along with a number of my colleagues, I was drawn to personal construct psychology as an approach which places any presenting problem firmly within the context of the personality as a whole: how people see themselves and how they construe the nature of their difficulty forms the central and most important aspect of our 'assessment', and the basis for any plans drawn up with them for amelioration.

Working initially with Fay Fransella in studying construct theory and its application to therapy, I later helped to set up the Centre for Personal Construct Psychology in London. Training courses were offered to people from a wide range of helping professions, and by 1982 a diploma course was established. By this time I was working with Centre clients – both children and adults – who had other than speech and language problems. This has remained the pattern of my counselling work ever since. Although for domestic reasons I am no longer a member of the Centre staff, I remain a consultant and work with students in teaching and supervision.

The lessons

During the past ten years I have learned many lessons about the intricacies of the counselling process, about the complexities of clients, and, perhaps most of all, about myself. The examples which follow illustrate a blend of failure fully to anticipate a person's response to a situation, and going against my intuitive understanding because of some overriding construction of my own. Here is an example of the latter.

Who referred whom, for what?

Ray, as I shall call him, made an appointment to see me, saying vaguely that 'a friend' had suggested I might be able to help him. My first mistake was to fail to ask Ray who that friend was, in response to his obvious reluctance to say. We had an initial meeting, at the end of which we agreed on some exploratory sessions, which would enable us to clarify aspects of the depression he complained of, and gain some idea of what a counselling series might involve for him. As always, I made it clear that I considered myself committed from this point, should he choose to go on, so there was no sense of the client's being 'on probation'.

The dilemma
When Ray began to tell his story in more detail at our next session, it emerged that the referrer was his girlfriend, Gill, with whom I had only recently ended a period of counselling. It had been understood between Gill and me that she could return if she felt the need. Given Ray and Gill's close relationship, I would not normally have taken on a potential ongoing client's partner unless they came together. People can become threatened as they realize the implications of each being discussed by the other, which can affect a client's openness, despite an agreement with regard to confidentiality.

My understanding of Gill suggested two possibilities which bothered me. First, although more confident in her sense of her own worth, she remained over-concerned about what others thought and said about her. She would know that I would not discuss her with Ray, but could become anxious about what he might say about her to me. Second, although Gill had come to recognize the need to control others, I could not be sure she had resolved this. Was there perhaps a message here to *make* Ray the kind of person she had always felt she needed?

On the other hand, it was clear from what he had said so far that Ray had a history of rejection. Would my saying he should see someone else be yet another one?

My second mistake was to leave it to Ray and Gill to look at the possible disadvantages of the arrangement, and, when they saw no real problems, to go ahead. There *was* trouble. There probably would have been difficulty for them both anyway, as the changes

Ray wanted in himself were likely to challenge certain vulnerable areas in Gill. But they could have been spared something if I had not allowed my concern for one aspect of the dilemma – Ray's experience of rejection – to govern my decision.

The consequences

One major source of difficulty was that Gill had shared the experience of her sessions with Ray, and she fully expected him to do the same. He, however, was not willing to discuss the content of our meetings, which made her feel shut out. Ray set about changing his behaviour towards Gill without warning, so that she became confused and angry. When he began to describe the quarrels which ensued, I tried to suggest ways in which he could make things less threatening for Gill, while still elaborating on the less dependent role he desired. The crunch came when Ray decided to apply for a promotion in the firm where they worked in the same department. Gill had been urging him to take this step for some time, but when Ray at last went ahead, the implications of their being separated and his being senior to her increased her anxiety.

Not surprisingly, Gill was furious with me. Fortunately, she arranged to come to see me. The session with her was a difficult one. She acknowledged that Ray's coming for counselling was her idea, and that she had been warned of possible problems. Nevertheless, she had not expected Ray to be so 'selfish' in his attempts to develop his own potential, and considered that I should have 'seen to it' that he shared his experience with her. We were able to make sense of her feelings, and to link them with old material we had worked on earlier. When Gill discussed this with Ray, he too was able to communicate more of what had happened and was happening now to him. Subsequently, they came to counselling together.

So what was new?

Before this I had been aware of the dangers of seeing two people who were in a close relationship for individual therapy. In this instance I went against my better judgement, largely to spare Ray from feeling personally rejected. We could, instead, have used my decision not to work with him as an opportunity for him to challenge such an old theory, and construe the event in more practical terms.

Since changes in a client will usually have some effect on those close to them, I see it as part of my responsibility to make sure the client is aware of this. Beyond that, what the client does about it is his or her responsibility. In this case, however, I was torn between concern for Gill, and not wanting to discourage Ray. I could have suggested that the three of us discuss this together, but I felt this might be too confronting for Ray at a fragile stage in his work. Once again, I deprived him of an opportunity to deal with threat.

During my own therapy I discovered a tendency to protect people, which recurred from very early days. The lesson here for me as a counsellor was that such a personal need could interfere with my professional judgement as to what was most helpful for clients. In this instance, it overrode the more important and far-reaching implications of working with Ray, and the possible effects this might have on Gill. Since then I believe I have been able to share such misgivings more openly with clients, and to work through any feelings of threat involved with them.

A client's rights

In the next example, I again had misgivings about a decision I felt I had to make on the spur of the moment. I have since learned to allow myself time to consider the implications of decisions more fully.

At about the time when the issue of clients and/or patients having access to their medical notes was first being debated, I was coming to the end of a counselling series with Clara. She had first presented with an eating disorder, and proved unusually responsive, given such a complex and often intractable area of difficulty. She was not severely overweight, and had become an expert in 'sensible nutrition' over the years. It seemed she needed the support of someone who took her seriously in order to find other ways of dealing with the fears and frustrations which caused her to overeat.

After a relatively short time we focused hardly at all on food and spent most of the sessions exploring various relationships, especially that with her mother. The details of this are not relevant here, but, in brief, it emerged that Clara was extremely ambivalent in her wish for independence from her mother, and her need to feel she was always there for her, which was also reflected in other relationships. Mainly through clarifying a balance of trust between the two of them, Clara managed to reduce her anxieties a good deal. We came to the last but one session.

The impulsive choice

Right at the end of the session, Clara asked whether she could read the notes I kept of the sessions. My immediate reaction was one of anxiety. I had nothing to hide in terms of content, which I had shared with her in discussion throughout; however, I had some doubts as to whether she would make sense of my concise style of note-making. As I could not think at that time of any good reason why she should not read the notes, I gave them to her.

Afterthoughts

When Clara had gone, however, I felt uneasy. I had not had time to explore why she wanted to see them. I tried to imagine what she would be looking for that she had been unable to ask me about directly. I had told her that next time we would make a final summary of what had developed during our sessions together; perhaps the notes were to help her construe the series as a whole? Was she more anxious than I realized about letting go of the supportive side of the relationship? I was almost sure that her dependencies were sufficiently dispersed among her husband and various other members of her family and friends for the relationship with me to be relatively easy to end.

I could come up with no answer, but I did reflect on what my alternatives might have been. To refuse outright, as if her request were in some way breaking professional boundaries, did not make sense; to have said I would need time to put them into a more legible and comprehensive form perhaps did.

Clara's reaction

Clara was furious – not because I had in any way kept things hidden from her or written things about her that she did not like, but because she had felt we had a warm relationship and my notes were 'cold' (which they would be, expressed as they were in key, telegrammatic phrases). She had felt depersonalized, seeing herself referred to as 'C', and so on. Although I felt duly chastened at not having anticipated this, and said so, it was important that we both learned something from it. Otherwise she would do as she had so often done in the past and end a relationship in high dudgeon, as if there were again no other way of separating.

Clara was able to acknowledge that her main reason for wanting to read my notes was to see whether she could trust her sense of having been not only understood but also 'genuinely liked' by me. This brought up for review a number of issues from the past about friendships, and, especially, whether her mother's concern for her came from some kind of duty or from real affection. By the end of the session we came to the conclusion that her reaction had indeed been to do with leaving counselling. Clara had expressed her satisfaction for some time at feeling able to go on without my support, and had ignored some deeper misgivings. I for my part had not paid enough attention to this latter aspect.

Nevertheless, we agreed to end as planned, with the proviso that she would return after a break if what she called her 'temporary lapse' proved to be more than an old way of dealing with things which she did not need any more.

The underlying lesson

The main lesson for me was again a personal one: I should have listened to my gut anxious reaction instead of making a spot decision to comply with Clara's wishes. I had pre-empted too quickly on a personal rather than a professional level, wanting to be seen as the sort of therapist who is 'open', rather than 'cagey', ready to respond to something 'new' rather than hemmed in by protocol, etc. This had overtaken a proper professional caution, which could at least have given me time to consider the implications in full. No one has asked to see my notes since. If they do, I will establish their reason and, if it seems useful for them to read them, explain the unvarnished nature of my note-taking.

If you don't ask . . .

In an initial interview with clients, I see my main task as listening and encouraging them to tell their story as it comes naturally to them. I then describe the personal construct approach, and, if they feel comfortable talking to me, agree on some initial sessions. A few questions are usually appropriate, but the one I failed to ask the next client had never occurred to me.

From time to time, every counsellor finds herself working with a client who seems determined to block all attempts to clarify their situation, let alone to help them to change it. Tony had stuttered since he was ten years old, and now, at the age of forty-two, having read an article I had written on the subject, said he would like to try the personal construct approach. I enquired what other therapy he had undergone, and was given a formidable list stretching over the past thirty years.

We discussed what Tony's expectations of yet another attempt to overcome his problem were. He had decided that his difficulty was 'psychological', and related to dependency on his ageing parents, which he resented bitterly but felt unable to loosen. Taking his speech problem in the context of himself as a whole person would, he hoped, make more sense than focusing on the disfluency alone.

The losing battle
It soon became clear that one of Tony's theories about life was
that everything conspired against him. As a Kellyan, I took his
'resistance' seriously. I recognized in his stream of evidence as to
the uselessness of speech therapy a desperate need to prove his
problems to be of such magnitude and complexity that no one
could possibly either understand or help. His mission in life seemed
to have been to sample one approach after another in order to
maintain this theory. Why?

Tony had begun to stutter on changing schools at the age of ten.
He had never forgiven his parents for that move. Nor could he
forgive them for not seeking help for his stuttering when it began,
which they hoped would 'go away'. Tony was an only child, and
looked to his mother to speak for him more and more as time went
on. He made no friends, and spent all his time in his parents'
company or alone.

He began to search for a 'cure' in his early twenties. There then
came a point when it seemed he had given up expecting therapy to
work, but needed to pit his wits against those who claimed to be
able to help. It was clear that the work required to unravel the
tangled tie with his parents would have to be long and deep. At this
early stage, however, when he had not committed himself to a
series, the explanation of such intensely core issues would be too
threatening. So I set about exploring his construing of change and
experiment.

I attempted to help Tony to elaborate the possibilities of expand-
ing his life and discovering what else he was besides a stutterer. I
tried to encourage him to review his notions about other people,
which largely revolved around what he saw as their reactions to his
stuttering. By the fifth session we had looked at issues of threat in
making changes, which exists for many people. We had explored
some of the disadvantages as well as the advantages he would
experience if he were free both to speak as he wished and to leave
his parents. Tony, however, had read all the books and knew
about 'pay-offs' and 'secondary gains'. I clearly had no understanding of his situation at all.

It was time to acknowledge to him that I was stuck too. Did that
mean he could not be helped? No. Only that until he felt more able
to challenge some of his ideas and feelings about himself and others,
I could see no way of making headway. He sat back and sighed.
What did I think he should do now? I asked him how it might be
if he gave his search a rest; if he turned his attention and energy to
something in life he had never tried before, which had nothing to do
with stuttering, and bore no relevance to his relationship with his

parents. He looked startled and replied, 'That's not what Wendy says!'

When I asked who Wendy was he blushed. Wendy was his 'other therapist'. Apparently he went to see her twice a week, and had been going for the last three years. Tony had wondered whether to tell me at our first meeting, but as I had not asked . . . Which was true. I had asked about former therapy, but it had not occurred to me to check whether he was seeing anyone currently. Had he not found it confusing? Not really; he had hoped that seeing two of us might be twice as effective! I had to reflect that he might also be proved doubly right in his view of the uselessness of all his attempts to find help.

What if I had known?
I wondered later what difference it would have made if I had known at our first session that Tony was already in therapy. I would have suggested that he discuss any dissatisfaction he might have directly with Wendy, before seeking help elsewhere. Might I have understood his entrenched position sooner and been able to give him more than I had during those five fruitless sessions? Perhaps not. I might have picked up the degree of his hostility, however, and used our one meeting to offer him an alternative view of what he was doing.

Since then I have always checked whether prospective clients are involved in counselling, or any other form of help elsewhere. Sometimes, of course, other approaches are quite compatible with a counselling series, for example, yoga, meditation, physical therapies, or other ways of enhancing a person's well-being. Occasionally a client has wanted to see me when unhappy with his current therapy or counselling, hoping to have somewhere to go before breaking the other tie. In each case I have referred people back to the counsellor or therapist involved.

Families and how not to survive them

The example which follows illustrates a counsellor's ongoing need to reflect on personal issues which might influence therapeutic decisions. In this case, whether to take on a client at all.

Francis was in his early twenties when he came to see me with his parents. He had some degree of physical disability, learning difficulties, and was quite withdrawn. He spoke very little, and was quite disfluent and hard to understand. It emerged that he was very close to and dependent on his mother. She seemed both desperately anxious about Francis's future, and impatient with his slowness.

His father was clearly ashamed of him, and regarded him as 'lazy' as well as 'dim'. Francis had had speech therapy, physiotherapy, and remedial teaching of various kinds, and now his parents wanted some help with his 'personality', which they regarded as undeveloped and socially unacceptable.

I knew from the beginning that I would be taking on far more than this young man's inevitable difficulties. It was clear that his mother had enormous problems of her own. I doubted whether the father would be prepared to modify his attitude; for years he had looked for someone to make his son 'normal'. They both seemed to want me to mould Francis into something he could not be, rather than to help him to find the resources he had within him. They had all rejected any links with handicapped people and other families in similar situations.

Going it alone
With so many issues involved, I should have waited to talk things through with my supervisor, but instead I suggested that, since they were all three very much involved, they might gain more from working as a family with myself and a colleague. Father dismissed the idea at once, and mother said that Francis should have my full attention. I made it clear that if Francis felt he would like to come on his own it would be for him to share what went on in the sessions if he wished. Mother was somewhat taken aback, but agreed. Francis said without very much enthusiasm that he would like to come. I felt very uneasy and rather inadequate.

The first few sessions with Francis were uphill work. He was not used to putting how he felt into words, and his poor hand-control ruled out drawing as a means of exploring his inner world. He had no friends and very few relatives, and could only speak of his parents in very concrete, physical terms. Gradually, he began to speak of his childhood in South Africa, and of one person who had been important to him – a nanny, whom he had not thought about for years. This led to his being more able to express some of the feelings he had about being a disappointment to his parents, and unable to share in so many things which others seemed to enjoy.

Then the phone calls from mother began. How could I help Francis to get a job? His table manners made it embarrassing when they had guests – what could I do about it? I explained, without giving any details, that the focus of the sessions was on how Francis saw things and what he felt he could do to change his approach to life. I offered to find out where he should go for advice on work, as he himself had touched on this. His mother sounded more and more desperate each time she telephoned, and it seemed from Francis that they were unable to communicate with each other, although he had tried.

We continued our sessions for about a year, and I think Francis gained something from becoming able to talk more openly about himself and construe other people more fully. But nothing changed very radically within the family, which was locked in a kind of angry dependency. Father put a stop to the series because it was not producing 'results'.

Knowing when to say 'no'

My experience, my training, and my intuition told me I could do little for Francis without some real involvement on the part of his parents, either with myself and a colleague, or with someone else with whom they could confront their own problems. So why did I agree to take him on? It was not, I think, some notion that I could perform miracles. Nor did I underestimate the force of Francis's parents' attitude or his own dependence on them. It was something personal interfering with my understanding as a professional. I, like many of my colleagues, find it hard to refuse when asked for help. This is not a virtue. The request must be weighed against the likelihood of a successful outcome. In those relatively early days of my counselling experience I had not learned when it was better for all concerned to say 'no'.

An issue of fees

It has been several years since I worked with the next client. Although I realized from the beginning that change would be difficult for her, I underestimated the extent to which her expectations of failure were governing her life.

It was clear that Daniella had constricted her life through the mishandling of money, among other things, for years. She was talented, and had been on the brink of many exciting opportunities but had backed off, leaving herself once more penniless. This left her feeling unable to socialize, trapped in solitude and inactivity. She saw this as the cause of her eating disorder – loneliness triggering off bingeing, followed by desperate attempts to lose weight, and so on, in the endless bulimic cycle.

The situation was far from as simple as this. Although it is not within the scope of this chapter to go into details of her complex difficulties, it became clear that it was Daniella's intense preoccupation with food, and the long-standing confusion and self-disgust that lay behind it, which spread a sense of chaos into every aspect of her life, including her handling of money.

As she was unemployed, when Daniella first came to counselling I charged her a very small fee. Gradually, through unravelling some of the threads of her traumatic history, and coming to challenge a number of theories as to her 'badness', Daniella began to discover what else she was besides bulimic and 'hopeless with money'. Things began to improve. Her eating was under control and less frightening; she had at last been accepted for a reasonable job; there was even the prospect of moving into a flat with a new friend.

The threat of change
I tried to help Daniella to prepare for changes before they occurred. We looked at the structure of the days to come, with work as their focus, and how it would feel to be surrounded by people again. We reviewed strategies to deal with moments of anxiety and pressure, as an alternative to reaching for food. She had taken her friend into her confidence, and felt supported and accepted for the first time in her life. We were both cautiously optimistic at our last meeting before Daniella was due to start her job.

Then her father arrived from America on a surprise visit. He criticized Daniella for the way she dressed, was far from encouraging about her ability to do the job, and took against her friend as being 'ordinary and dull'. This was not what Daniella needed at this time. She telephoned me on the Sunday evening, saying she could not make it the next day as she felt too upset. After a long conversation, during which I tried to remind her of how far she had come and all she had planned to do to cope, she agreed to go in to work and to try to leave her father and his negative influence behind.

When I saw Daniella two days later, she looked dreadful. She had managed the first day, but had then spent the evening with her father, who had told her how hard it had been when she was a child, trying to do his best for her, with her mother drinking and seeing other men. It brought back all her old terrors and feelings of guilt, and when her father left, she ate everything she could lay her hands on. She was then sick all night, and telephoned work to say she would not be coming back.

I asked Daniella whether she could possibly view what had happened as other than her own abject failure; to consider what she had been up against, and whether anyone at this stage could have been unaffected by the old messages and her father's destructive way of dealing with his own unhappiness. By the end of the session Daniella agreed to go on, but I felt even then that she had little hope.

In the few sessions that followed, Daniella was very dispirited. Losing the job meant she could not move in with her friend, and very soon she was broke again. She could not come to counselling any more. I said it was her choice, but I hoped she would. I had what I thought was a brilliant idea for solving the problem of payment for a while at least: Daniella had shown me some of her sketches, which were very skilled, and I asked her whether she would like to pay for some sessions with drawings I needed for a child I was working with. She seemed relieved and enthusiastic, and made notes of what I wanted. But the next time she came she looked crestfallen. She had not been able to do any drawing. She had simply 'blocked'. She would not hear of my waiving the fees for a while or waiting until she was able to pay; she would get in touch when she had sorted herself out. I wrote a while later to ask how she was getting on, but I never heard from Daniella again.

When change is too difficult

I was left with much heart-searching. If Daniella's father had not come over at that time, would she have been able to build up her sense of her own worth to withstand his negative influence? Did going on after she had come to say goodbye do more harm than good? And was the offer of her doing the drawings adding insult to injury? I shall never know whether it was a big mistake or just a fruitless try.

This sad episode has not helped with the problem many of us have with the whole question of private practice. My home situation makes this the best way to work as a counsellor. Operating a sliding scale of fees in an attempt to respond to people's differing circumstances, seems the fairest thing to do. Having a set fee which clients can take or leave is undoubtedly the simplest. I still have a sliding scale, but I do explore the issue of payment more carefully with clients who have problems handling money. Where possible, for example, with a client in Daniella's situation, I would direct her for help to an organization which does not charge for counselling. This may mean waiting, but the risk of the client's losing the impetus to change is no greater than the risk of ending so unsatisfactorily.

Conclusion

Most of these examples of hard-learned lessons show that for me, at least, mistakes occur when an aspect of my construing of myself interferes with what would otherwise be my professional judgement.

In the case of Ray and Gill I had a dilemma around my old image of myself as one who must protect people: should I face Ray with the threat of rejection, or possibly expose Gill to the anxiety of knowing she was being discussed by Ray? To leave the decision to them was to avoid the issue.

With Clara, it was my view of myself as 'open' and 'responsive' which led me to hand over my notes, without giving myself time to explore the situation and reflect on the possible outcome. I had understood her difficulty in believing that others cared for her, and should have realized that she would look for evidence of this in what I had written.

Working with Daniella involved two important personal issues for me: the problem I have in relation to fees, and my reluctance to give up when a client is plainly telling me that change is too difficult. I still need to work on the first, but on reflection, in this instance the second is probably more significant. For years Daniella had sabotaged all her attempts to free herself from her eating disorder. She hated it, but it was the only way she knew of making her world predictable. That way she was at least in control of her pattern of failure, of which the counselling series was only a small part.

There is a clear link between my reluctance to give up and my failure to refuse to work with Francis on his parents' terms. Here, though, it was clear from the beginning that my efforts were doomed. There was an alternative, which I might well still take, to turning someone down outright and experiencing the guilt this would involve. This would have been to make a contract for a certain number of sessions, to see whether what I had to offer in those circumstances would help. This is my usual practice these days, but at the time I was new to counselling and still influenced by my old ways of pressing on, regardless.

Longer experience with counselling has also shown me the importance of supervision. I had none as a speech therapist, and I believe there is little offered to them now. In three of these instances, mistakes could have been avoided if I had delayed taking a decision and discussed the implications with a supervisor. In supervision we share not only our approach to counselling with a colleague, but enough of ourselves for him or her to alert us to interference with professional judgement coming from personal issues.

3 Emmy van Deurzen-Smith

It is hard to admit that your counselling work is sometimes harmful rather than helpful. It is even harder to see what exactly you do wrong. It is hardest of all to actually learn from your mistakes, and to put the experience to positive use. Only time will allow you genuinely to reap the benefits of new insights and to implement them in your work. People can take many years to assimilate new ideas, and counsellors are no exception to the rule.

While preparing to write this chapter about some of my own mistakes, I was struck by how much I could learn from events long past. The wisdom hidden in each situation is released in small doses as and when we are ready to read the message; lessons drawn from the same experience will vary over time, according to the new perspectives we acquire. The key to learning, however, remains the same in all situations: that of candid reappraisal. One has to give up the proud belief in one's own knowledge and expertise, and accept situations in all their embarrassing detail and complexity.

I offer the following illustrations of my personal struggles with an overriding sense of relief at speaking the unspeakable. I have tried to set the learning in context without finding blame, either in myself, in others, or in situations. My own quest for answers, and my discovery of questions is illustrated in the following case examples, encompassing twenty years of counselling work. If I have learnt anything during that time it is to have a greater capacity to spot errors, and to sustain my own and other people's scrutiny of them.

Death: the great supervisor

My first experience of therapeutic work took place within the setting of psychiatric hospitals, where I undertook counselling, first in a voluntary and then in a professional capacity. I was in my early twenties, and had studied philosophy rather than psychology, although psychoanalysis had been included in the curriculum. My attitude to my work was one of great optimism, and I had more than my fair share of missionary zeal. I saw counselling as an opportunity to make the world a better place, and I was filled with the conviction that it was possible to help people straighten out their lives no matter how confused or perturbed they were.

The first hospital in which I had a full-time post was located in the middle of the French Massif Central. It had been a place of revolutionary progress, which is why I sought it out. It was the first psychiatric hospital in France to break down its walls, and allow all patients to come and go as they wished. As the hospital was situated in the mountains, with no major urban centres within a radius of 100 miles, there was little incentive for people to run away. On the contrary, there was all reason for them to remain as the hospital was organized with a communal structure, enabling patients to participate actively in all aspects of its life. Some of them were in positions of leadership in the print shop, the woodwork shop, the kitchens, or the laundry. Others were instrumental in the social activities which were the centre of the hospital and village life.

With so little cultural activity in the area, the hospital was the point of reference for the staff as much as for the patients. During the two years I was resident, I spent most of my evenings talking and drinking, dancing, organizing games, or playing boules with patients, doctors, and nurses. It was a fascinating time, and I learnt a tremendous amount from my personal relations with patients and staff alike. Just observing the senior therapists interacting with the patients taught me more than I had previously learnt through any other form of training.

Some patients had been there so long that they liked taking the new counsellor aside to teach her about their problems and how to get a handle on them. The camaraderie was great, and I was at the receiving end of a mixture of old-fashioned respect for someone with a university degree on the one hand, and parental concern for someone still so young and inexperienced on the other. On the whole this made for a fairly comfortable learning environment.

There were times when things were less rosy, and I was forced to confront my own naïvety and ignorance. One of the reasons for this was that I had been catapulted into a role of leadership for which I was not yet ready. As the wife of one of the five psychiatrists in the hospital, and with my philosophy degree and two years psychiatric work behind me, I was expected to fill the gap left by a previous registrar's wife. She had been a group analyst, and she and her husband had been the linchpins of the hospital's progressive therapeutic community programme.

Among other things, the doctor and his wife had created a hospital radio station and a weekly newsletter. Through these media anyone could say anything, no matter how controversial or offensive, on the condition that they come to the weekly meeting, where the issues were aired and discussed as the newsletter articles were read aloud and commented upon. These two-hour meetings

took place on Saturday mornings, and were the occasion for intensive sessions of group therapy. Fifty to eighty patients usually
attended, accompanied by perhaps five nurses and three psychiatrists. The social therapy centre, which was responsible for
organizing the meetings, was staffed by three counsellors, two of
whom had had intensive training with the therapists who had
created the system. Within weeks of my joining the team I was
asked to take over the management of the meetings, and I accepted
with a mixture of pride and trepidation. It really was a case of
fools rushing in where angels fear to tread.

Although the other staff and the registrars were usually quite
active at these meetings, and although we had regular debriefing
sessions afterwards, I often felt terribly exposed and sometimes
unable to bring difficult situations to their best conclusion. The
human distress and upset that was revealed in the newsletter
articles was such that I felt constantly pushed to the edge of my
human security. I used to tremble with anxiety every Saturday
morning, and it was only my strong desire to do well that allowed
me to believe that no matter how terrible the patient's situation,
there always was some way to understand and tackle it.

Interventions by most of the team were based on a mixture of
psychodynamic principles and common sense (the latter flavoured
strongly with the rough and ready morality of the French country-
side). There was also some psychodramatic input, and sometimes a
more directive behavioral one. The trend was to challenge people,
and encourage them to take charge of their own problems and speak
their minds. I easily became convinced that shaking people out of
their complacency was generally a good thing, as I often saw them
finding a more satisfactory place in the communal life after having
a go at writing a newsletter article and having their difficulties
publicly confronted.

Nevertheless, there were numerous occasions when I was shocked
at the way in which particular patients were brutalized by this rather
forthright way of tackling very private matters, and I had a tendency
to smooth ruffled feathers and ease tensions with rather moralistic
and calming remarks. I did not have the poise to conduct the
sessions with the authority required to keep people's emotions on an
even keel. I doubted my own insights, and pandered somewhat to
the greater knowledge and experience of the senior therapists, who
criticized me for being too intellectual, too scrupulous, and too
guarded in my approach. They rightly considered me naïve,
idealistic, and unequal to the task of dishing out home truths in the
way they believed was necessary. To them I was the privileged,
learned stranger from the city who needed toughening up.

There was undoubtedly some truth to this view, and given this context I felt self-conscious about my role as counsellor. At the same time I was aware that my youth and sensitivity – as well as my sense of alienation as a foreigner – made me more able to appreciate the experience of the most withdrawn patients. I felt far better equipped than many of my colleagues to understand some of the young schizophrenics who were often sent down to us from Parisian hospitals as a last resort.

In one-to-one work I trusted my own insights and abilities with these people. But the public group sessions, with their culture of questioning and confrontation, were a different matter. I was acutely aware that the interpretations offered were relative to the background of the therapist, but even so I did not have the strength or confidence to balance the interventions made with those based on my own perceptions. I needed some proof of the validity of my views before I would feel at ease with them and ready to stand by them. The proof that I needed came in a very costly manner.

One Saturday morning, as I was going over the articles that were up for discussion at the meeting, my attention was drawn by the writing of one of the regular contributors. Marcel was a very withdrawn, intellectual young man, who had been sent down to the hospital from a private clinic in Paris, where he had been unable to make progress. He usually wrote dry and totally impersonal articles that seemed to warrant very little discussion other than an invitation to express himself more personally. But today, instead of describing the beauty of the Roquefort region, Marcel had mentioned his personal preoccupations, describing his dismay at his parents' disapproval of his relationship with Sophie, another patient from Paris.

Marcel and Sophie had been seen walking hand-in-hand around the hospital for months now, and everyone considered them a steady, though somewhat oddly assorted, couple. They seemed to love each other madly in spite of what Marcel's parents considered to be an incompatibility of their social backgrounds. He was from a well-to-do family, and she was a simple working-class girl. Now that his parents had officially disapproved of the relationship and had told their son to put an end to it, Marcel wrote in the newsletter to announce this fact in quite a melodramatic way.

Predictably, he was forcefully challenged by some of the therapists to speak his own mind rather than hide behind his parents' views. Rather than helping him to articulate his own views, this entrenched him in a defensive position. Sophie, who was also present at the meeting, was visibly shaken by the situation, and I felt an urgency to let her viewpoint be heard too. I drew her into the discussion, intending to help her express her sadness at being abandoned. She was not able to master the force of her own and Marcel's emotions, however, and joined in with the general tendency to speak scathingly to Marcel. Before long a violent quarrel had started between Marcel and Sophie, each shouting in mad anger at the other. I was at a loss to handle the situation tactfully, and felt rather overwhelmed by the force of the emotions at play.

Some of the other therapists responded with excited exhortations to both Marcel and Sophie to tell each other the truth about their feelings at last. I was aware that many of my colleagues considered the situation a breakthrough for both patients, who were finally expressing feelings which were normally held very tightly in check. My intuitive sense was that this was no positive gain, and that destructive forces were at work that could eventually only confirm these two in their usual state of withdrawal. However, I did not have the confidence to trust myself. Even if I had, I would not have had the authority to bring an explosive situation back under control.

Marcel worked himself up to unexpected levels of hateful and furious abuse of Sophie in a pathetic attempt to show everyone how he himself, not his parents, dismissed her as a possible partner. He called her the most odious names and aired all his frustrations with her; he threatened her physically to make her leave the room. Sophie, though giving as good as she got up to a point, was finally cowed into marching out in anger. No one dared intervene. The therapeutic culture interpreted the situation as an achievement; Marcel was even congratulated on having spoken his mind at last. I felt like a failure for not having been able to keep the situation in perspective, but I let myself be convinced by my colleagues that I was too soft, and that I should learn to actively bring about such situations regularly.

It was not until later that evening that people began to worry about Sophie, who had not come back to her ward. Late that night, a search party was sent out to look for her. By six o'clock the next morning, Sophie's stiffened body was found in a nearby swamp. Accidental death was recorded: she had wandered into dangerous territory and had slipped. The metaphor seemed cynical and tragically appropriate to what my memory had recorded. To me this was no accident: I felt deeply guilty for having stood by and let her be challenged to death.

Others too did some soul-searching as the post-mortem meetings went over the facts again and again. But the fault was generally seen to lie nowhere in particular, or perhaps mostly with Marcel's parents. People were not willing to really question the therapeutic methods that had been employed. It was only over the months and years to come that I reclaimed my guilt and started to draw some conclusions. All the supervision I had on this case tended to whitewash my role and minimize the responsibility of any of us who had been there that day. Taking responsibility meant questioning the whole set-up of the hospital. Even Sophie's death did not appear to warrant such a price.

I found I could not progress in my professional development until I questioned my own role in this tragedy. I needed to face my previous lack of understanding of the large group process before I could start noticing some of the forces that had been at work. I needed to recognize the narrowness of my thinking about human emotions before I could begin to make sense of the apparent contradictions of the events of the day. I needed to acknowledge how I had held back from intervening, even though my intuition told me clearly what was wrong and what would be right. I vowed I would develop the necessary strength to stand by my intuitions.

Most importantly, I needed to accept that I had, by my own standards, failed miserably to be in charge of the group meeting: for only then was I free to begin to recognize and define my professional values and goals. I discovered there was a force of complacency and inertia in others and myself that inclined us to shirk all responsibility. Everyone was protecting everyone else from learning anything from the situation at all; it seemed easier to soothe the pain of Sophie's death by pretending it had been inevitable. I found in the end I preferred the pain of feeling some responsibility for my failure, for it alone could lead to the hope that I could also have a positive impact and become truly effective in my work.

I learnt that if I were to embark upon such a road I needed to sharpen my theoretical knowledge and understanding of the human predicament, as well as gain lots more personal and professional experience and grow stronger and more insightful. Without this I could not work to the level which I knew myself capable of working to. I also decided I would rely less upon human opinion to guide my work and more upon the facts of life. The reality of Sophie's death had proved to be the ultimate and only supervisor worth relying upon.

Knee-deep into regression

After those first few intensive years of learning the profession, I decided to go back to university to get a first degree in psychology and a masters degree in clinical psychology. I had moved to a new hospital: less experimental in nature, but equipped to provide me with more intensive and in-depth, one-to-one work, as well as regular supervision with a well-known Lacanian psychoanalyst. I also attended seminars in psychiatry and psychotherapy offered through Bordeaux University, which introduced me to the use of phenomenology in psychotherapy (Binswanger, 1962; Boss, 1957). This brought together my previous philosophical research with my clinical practice, and set me on the track of my future pursuit to base counselling and psychotherapy on a firm philosophical foundation.

With the accumulating weight of experience and training, I began to experiment with new counselling methods that were in line with the approach that most interested me: anti-psychiatry. One of the problems with working in an anti-psychiatric manner was that the work of Laing (1960, 1961, 1967) and Cooper (1967) said practically nothing about practical application, and so the descriptions of regression work in Barnes and Berke's book (1973) became the only available guideline.

Much of my counselling in the new hospital emphasized couple and family work. My then husband and I worked as a psychiatrist–psychologist team, and we did much of the counselling and therapeutic work together, taking many novel initiatives within the hospital. We inevitably came to a rude awakening as we experimented with new methods without quite knowing what we were playing with.

We had just started to work with Hélène, a young mother of two, who had arrived at the hospital after a serious suicide attempt. She was deeply depressed, but very eager to take up the counselling sessions I offered to her after the initial assessment interviews and tests. It soon became obvious that she experienced her relationship to her husband as a major obstacle in her life. She felt incapable of coping with his demands on her as a woman, a wife, and a mother.

It was decided by the team that couple counselling would be more helpful, and my ex-husband and I saw the two for numerous sessions, both together and separately. Soon Hélène was able to leave the hospital in a much more optimistic frame of mind, while continuing to return with her husband for twice-weekly marital counselling sessions. Her husband, however, began to feel increasingly threatened in these sessions. This was hardly surprising as it must have been quite obvious that both counsellors believed he needed to make some important adjustments to accommodate his wife's weakness and needs.

With hindsight, I think we sided unashamedly with the perceived victim in the situation, who, after all, was our patient. While intending to help her become more independent, we encouraged her to evaluate the situation as untenable. The husband was rather insensitive, and was also occasionally violent to her and the children, so it was difficult to like him. Nevertheless, it would have been preferable to have tried harder to get to the bottom of his frustrations. Instead, we more or less dismissed his desire to see his wife behave 'more normally' as he used to put it. We naturally and wrongly assumed we needed to protect her, and made that clear in our interventions. The whole situation was a good example of how one's theoretical and personal beliefs bias one's views of the situation, and, therefore, one's interventions.

The couple counselling finished before long as Hélène and her husband decided to begin divorce proceedings. We were a bit taken aback by this rapid development, and questioned ourselves vigorously on what the couple might be acting out for us. None of this questioning threw much light on the situation, as nobody – including our supervisor and other colleagues – had an inkling of the developments that were soon to follow, and that we had undoubtedly ourselves helped to shape.

As soon as Hélène lost her husband's support, she turned to her counsellors to rescue her. None of this was rational or explicit: she simply collapsed and had to be hospitalized yet again. But this time she let herself go into a deep state of regression, clamouring for our continuous and sustained care and attention. To our dismay we saw her lose all control over her own emotions, throwing tantrums, going manic, getting withdrawn, and so on. Eventually she remained in her bed, soiling herself and needing to be spoon-fed.

I was seeing her nearly every day, but formal counselling sessions were out of the question. Our anti-psychiatric notions were being put to the test sharply, as we were tempted to resort to simple psychiatric diagnoses and treatment to fix the situation and make Hélène behave 'more normally', exactly as the husband had wanted. There was a time when Hélène went mute and refused to communicate directly to anyone. Nevertheless, she stood close by when the team discussed her, and threw a shoe at us when we talked about her in what she perceived as a demeaning manner.

I tried at first to have patience with her regression, but the fact was that it did not seem right or necessary for her to be in such a terrible state of dilapidation, no matter what the anti-psychiatry books suggested. The nurses did not appreciate the constant hassle and extra work, and they were very concerned about her psychotic state. I gradually became convinced that the counselling had to take a new direction. Rather than helping her to get in touch with more and more intense levels of feelings, and rather than helping her make connections with past experiences of her sense of inadequacy and inability to communicate, I began to talk to her about life and how to survive it.

There is little doubt that I improvised desperately and furiously in order to get out of what I instinctively sensed to be a potentially lethal failure of my own work and Hélène's life. I abandoned all the professional timidity that used to hamper my work. I no longer tried to make interpretations or reflect back, or show empathy of any kind. I merely spoke my mind, and in the process accused myself of having encouraged her to regress in this way. Somehow Hélène saw the reality behind my words and grasped the urgency of my meaning. I refused to see her so often any longer, and resumed seeing her twice weekly, urging her to come to the counselling room again instead of lingering on the ward. The whole team was in agreement with this new line, and we weaned Hélène off her regression in weeks.

Over the next months she behaved like an adolescent girl discovering her own budding maturity, and became involved with another patient in the hospital in a very intense manner. It was eventually decided it would be best for her to go to a halfway house for young women, rather than try to live on her own with her children. It seemed that Hélène really did need to find a way to stand alone in the world before she could tackle all the demands of adult life. When I left the hospital she was established in her new life with a fair amount of confidence. Even so, I wondered whether the situation could not have been handled more effectively at an earlier stage, reducing the losses she and her children suffered in the process.

My trials with Hélène had a great impact on me. It was only gradually that I could admit to myself all the doubts I had about my work with her. The experience taught me the importance of a sober and sound appraisal of a client's predicament, and the value of finding a personal and level-headed way to intervene, based upon a realistic rather than an idealistic view of the world.

I also discovered that the encouragement of regression may be based upon and inspired by a counsellor's desire to be needed and to have a visible impact. I came to see regression as often counterproductive, and largely a function of one's inability to help the client to cope with difficulties more constructively.

Therapeutic delusions

Not long after my experience with Hélène, I decided to leave the hospital environment to come and work in London with the proponents of anti-psychiatry. I wanted to find out how to handle situations like this more expertly, and to learn as much as I could from the only professionals I still admired for their controversial writing.

My ex-husband and I were invited to come and work within a residential therapeutic community and to do some work at a crisis centre. In the process I learnt that my remaining illusions about professionals' privileged knowledge and insight into people's suffering were indeed illusions. This experience also confirmed my view that it is important to intervene on the basis of one's insight into life and from a sense of one's own struggles with life: in other words, from a personal rather than a theoretical position.

It was my work with Philip that was the turning point of my understanding. Philip was a lecturer in his sixties. He had a breakdown during his holiday in London, and had walked naked in the streets and shouted at people in the public library. He was in a state of great upset and excitement. He did not want to be locked up in a mental hospital, but he recognized that he needed some assistance. When he arrived at the crisis centre, he had mixed feelings about the place. He insisted that the people there did not understand him, or appreciate the fact that the world was on the edge of disaster.

Philip was preoccupied with time going by, and was convinced that the world was going to come to an end soon if he was not able to rescue it. He would call emergency services or stop people on the street to let them know they needed to help him to save the world. On one occasion he tried to set fire to the crisis centre. His presence was extremely disturbing and frightening to another guest at the centre, and it was exhausting to the residential therapists, as Philip did not sleep at night at all. It was because of this that my ex-husband and I were called in, to relieve the team and to help with the sort of behaviour that we had a lot of previous experience dealing with during our years of work in mental hospitals.

When we arrived, Philip had finally gone to bed for a rest. There was an atmosphere of terror in the house, and the therapists told us they did not think it wise to try and keep Philip going any longer without medication or hospitalization. Besides the residential therapists, there was a team of two therapists who worked with Philip in daily individual therapy sessions. These sessions were conducted in a neo-Kleinian fashion, with strong and repeated interpretations concerning Philip's desire to destroy the breast out of envy of his mother. His fear of the imminent end of the world was linked by the therapists to his fear of retaliation from the father. As we began to spend hours and hours with Philip, we were to gain direct insights into his own evaluation of these interpretations. We were to find ourselves interacting directly, without the protection of a professional role, with Philip's bright, inquiring, and critical mind.

Our first encounter with Philip occurred as he stumbled down the stairs, head first, as if he were trying to kill himself. He said he had gone blind and had fallen down helplessly. Over the next two days he was to maintain this blindness, as if he was shielding himself from having to face the world around him. It turned out to be a device that became the linchpin of his coming to terms with his distress. While the official therapist team interpreted Philip's blindness as a denial of his oedipal desires for his mother, Philip was much more interested in discussing with us the far-fetched nature of such an interpretation. The idea that he had fancied his mother and felt aggressive towards his father was neither familiar nor helpful to Philip, but the oedipal metaphor used in a more concrete sense was. As someone well versed in Greek mythology, Philip was quite ready to recognize the connection between Oedipus blinding himself when he could not cope with the facts of life, and his own temporary blindness.

He asked us to help him to write a manifesto to be put out in all public libraries, announcing the need for all mankind to work together in order to stop the world from being destroyed. Then he burnt the manifesto with us, asking us to make sure we would 'burn the I's' that figured in it. We laughed with him about the implications of what he was saying: that the personal – or the eyes – had to be sacrificed, in order to achieve the saving of mankind. It was clear that although Philip resented his own impotence in not being able to do more about the state of the world, he also recognized the need to move away from a strictly personal perspective on this dilemma. Rather like Oedipus, who made a personal sacrifice in order to save Thebes, Philip was seeking to find a way to be significant to mankind in the face of the nuclear, and other, threats that he felt so acutely aware of.

Making interpretations to Philip about his personal guilt in relation to his father and mother was not helpful. He would come out of his therapy sessions with the Kleinians, full of fury against their neglect of his personal meanings. He would fume and glare and say he did not want to screw his mother, and did not therefore feel guilty about this. But when I gently suggested that he did obviously feel guilty about some things, he would come back to a calmer mood and a willingness to explore his real guilt and sense of impotence in saving mankind.

We discovered together that awareness of guilt implies understanding about right and wrong, and therefore also shows a way forward for the future. It slowly began to dawn on him that there might be more constructive things to do than blinding himself, setting fire to a house, or getting undressed in the street. He began to search for more positive ways of having an impact, especially in relation to his teaching job.

It was obvious that Philip craved the ordinary dialogue that took place between us, exploring the things that mattered to him and from his point of view. He was scathing about the so-called 'deep psychotherapeutic work' he was going through at the same time, for it seemed to him this denied his reality and skated over the surface of his experience in order to make interpretations that seemed alien and clichéd.

It was in my work with Philip that I learnt to be true to what emerges in sessions with the client without trying to fit it into pre-established frames of reference. The struggle with Philip convinced me at last that I had to take this unmarked road with clients instead of relying on the theories in books. As is so often the case in working closely with clients, it was my daring to go on Philip's journey with him that marked a change in my own life. When Philip was ready to face life again in a different and more courageous manner, bringing his discontent about the world into his professional life rather than letting it oppress him, I was close to doing the same thing.

What this meant was that I had to strike out on my own, away from the comfort of the institutions within which I had thus far practised. This move to independence would hold its own challenges, and brought with it a whole new set of lessons to be learnt.

Unexpected limitations

In my personal life, some important changes took place at this stage: my ex-husband and I decided to separate after a year of intense crisis, and I opted to remain in Britain to work in private practice rather than remain in the therapeutic community and crisis centre or return to work in psychiatric hospitals. It was important to me to have the freedom to work in the manner I believed was right, and I was fortunate in also finding a lecturing job where I could begin voicing, exploring, and testing my ideas.

In this way I gradually worked out my own approach to the

psychotherapeutic dialogue, which I began to call existential counselling. Of course, there were many ups and downs in my work with private clients, but there was a definite sense that I was connecting with their true concerns. The trick, I found, was to balance a willingness to immerse myself in their preoccupations, with a retention of adequate boundaries in order to remain in charge and sane in the process. I got the hang of it quite well after a while.

What helped tremendously was to have brought my life in line with my beliefs and convictions, and to have lived, alone, through the challenges that this involved me in. When I met David, who was to become my second husband and the father of my children, it was like a conformation of being on the right path. Our relationship strengthened my sense of personal balance and security in such a way that my professional work improved more dramatically than it had done through any form of training. I felt increasingly on top of my work, and ready to tackle almost anything.

Then my personal lifestyle brought me up against my limitations. It was my own desire to have a baby that shook me out of my growing complacency. After ten years of professional work I discovered that my devotion to my clients could suddenly come up against a whole new set of priorities, with tremendous consequences for what I would be prepared to offer them.

I had taken it for granted that I would work from my home with people who needed intense work and great attention, which I had no hesitation in providing even though I always stuck to simple rules of time and space. When I became pregnant for the first time and began to feel tired, egocentric, and inclined to retreat, I was working with one particular client who made me wonder whether I could cope.

Yet when I decided to refer a number of my existing clients on to other therapists and counsellors because I wanted to cut down on the work I was doing, I kept Anne on because she seemed to need me more than the others. With hindsight this should have been the more reason to refer her on. Of all my clients, it was Anne who would cope least well with my pregnancy and childbirth. But it was my own inexperience as a mother that made it impossible to oversee the consequences of this decision.

When I was eight months pregnant, Anne became restless and concerned about my impending absence. She had been referred to me after a breakdown and spell in a psychiatric hospital, and had begun to worry about not being able to cope again when I moved to a larger flat half-way through my pregnancy. With my impending absence to deliver the baby, the scene was set for Anne to plunge into a second breakdown. She held herself together while I took a couple of weeks off to have my baby, and when I returned to my work with her she collapsed.

The mistake I made was not to recognize that Anne needed alternative arrangements. I thought I could handle seeing her up to the week of the birth and again almost immediately after. But though I did not miss more than two weeks of work (mainly because my work was my only source of income, and I could not afford to take a longer break), the quality and amount of attention I had to offer so soon after the birth of my son was nowhere near what Anne needed. Anne herself was a divorced, childless woman in her late thirties, whose difficulties centred around a sense that she had failed to do anything worthwhile with her life.

Behind her feminist and career-minded façade, Anne deeply hankered for a baby of her own. Her marriage had ended in disaster, and her boyfriend did not believe in family life. She had banned the idea of procreation from her list of desires, blatantly unaware of her own instincts. My new motherhood threw up many bad memories for Anne, who was the eldest of nine siblings, and brought out her own desires to be looked after. Her feelings of helplessness overwhelmed her, and I was useless because I felt myself overwhelmed by the demands of both my baby and my client. I wanted her to be grown-up and independent, while she wanted mothering from me. In addition, she was caught in the conflict between her suppressed wish to mother, and her blatant desire to be mothered. I was at a loss to help her sort it out at that particular time, because I was myself too caught up in a similar paradox, wishing I could be looked after so that I could look after my baby properly.

Anne was prematurely forced by the situation to face some painful issues that she might otherwise have been able to tackle more gradually. She was also deprived of her already fragile sense of being able to rely upon others, and she felt unable to cope alone.

She spent some weeks in a psychiatric hospital, during which time I did not visit her or speak to her once, as I needed the break as much as she did. When she returned she was frail, but willing to take a hard look at what had happened. We worked together for a further year, in twice-weekly sessions, making steady progress and coming to some understanding of the way in which she interacted with the world.

Then, when I moved to a different area, she chose to be referred on to a colleague. I did not go out of my way to offer her alternative arrangements to suit her well enough to make continuation possible. For although we had made considerable headway, and she had moved to a position of much greater self-understanding and security, there was a shared sense of relief that she could now make a fresh start with a new therapist.

The lesson I learnt from this experience was that it is crucial to not overestimate your own abilities, and that no matter how stable and experienced you feel there will always be new life experiences that will shake you out of your world in such a way as to question all of your previous learning. If the issues you are newly confronted with dovetail with those of your client, then extra caution and supervision are needed.

Personally, I concluded that I needed to cut my counselling work to much more reasonable proportions while my children were young and while I also had considerable teaching commitments. I chose to indicate those limitations to future clients and focus on shorter-term work. I discovered this to have a positive effect on the work itself: freeing me of unnecessary pressures and responsibilities and making the framework so clear to clients that their motivation to get on with the work seemed greatly improved as a consequence.

Blind spots

As my work has developed and I have matured, things which once seemed mysterious and difficult now often seem familiar and straightforward. As in every other profession, we tend to reach plateaus where it seems we can oversee the whole of our professional territory. Of course such complacency is inevitably challenged by encounters with unforeseen circumstances. Totally new aspects of old familiar issues can be revealed when you least expect it, and before you know it you have been bamboozled by a new mystery.

I now look forward to such moments of being stuck temporarily, having understood that they signify the new opportunities to rediscover my own ignorance and the endless variations of human experience. I find it rewarding when such a situation occurs in my own counselling work rather than in supervising students and trainees, as this is inevitably closer to home and involves the shining of light in my own blind spots rather than in those of others.

My recent experience with Teresa is a good example of such a discovery, and the removal of a personal blind spot that stood in the way of my client's progress towards understanding of her predicament.

Teresa was a mother in her forties, who came to counselling upon recommendation of her GP after years of struggles with her son Tony. Tony had lost the last years of his secondary schooling because of severe states of depression, which had been diagnosed as schizophrenia after he had to spend a couple of months in a psychiatric ward. Teresa had a deep sense of guilt about her son's difficulties, as he had begun to withdraw and get depressed around the time that her marriage to Tony's father was beginning to break up.

Teresa was sure that Tony had been disturbed by the constant fights between her and her husband Richard, and she was worried that she had needed her son's affection too much when Richard had not been there any longer for her. Because of this she had encouraged Tony to live with his dad after he returned from hospital: she hoped to make up for her possessive love of her son by sending him back to the father he had missed so much.

In the counselling sessions we went over her sense of having failed and of emotionally abusing her son. Both Teresa and I were used to Laingian ideas, and we operated from the implicit assumption that disturbance in children is often related to the pressure on them from their parents. I unquestionably assumed that she might indeed have been harmful to her son, even though I am generally sceptical of the current fashion of seeing child abuse everywhere. I helped her to work on gaining autonomy, and we focused on her strong attachment to her own mother. The problem with and alienation from her son, however, persisted. We were somehow missing the point.

Teresa dutifully tried to keep herself distant from her son and let him be free of her, and she reported instances of her struggles in doing so, against her better instincts. She seemed to expect approval from me at such moments, and it became evident to me that she was operating from the belief that I wanted her to behave in certain ways. It also became more and more clear that such behaviour did nothing for her, and nothing for her son.

It was only when she reported that her son had become extremely angry with her one day over a petty incident that the scales fell from my eyes. How could I have missed the paradox in the situation? How could I have been so blind to the obvious deceit in the relationship?

One look at what was actually in front of us revealed much more than all our previous attempts at analyzing the situation: here was Teresa, desperate with held-back love and longing for her son, anxiously avoiding any expression of her care and concern for fear of damaging the child further; and here was Tony, lonely and ill-at-ease at his father's, assuming that his mother had wanted to get rid of him because he had been too much to cope with for her on her own.

Tony had never once complained that he had suffered from his mother's need of him. It was worth checking what he had in fact experienced. Not surprisingly, it turned out that Tony actually felt that his mother's love, when it had flowed to him, had on the contrary kept him alive and hopeful in the face of the fights and divorce between his parents. It was only when he perceived his mother as rejecting him that he began to feel deprived and insecure.

When Teresa began to show her affection to Tony, plucking up the courage to reveal her struggles and doubts to him, Tony began trusting her enough to tell her about his predicament over the past years. He had identified with his father and had withdrawn into himself as his father withdrew from the house. He had seen his mother's attempts at not imposing her love on him as a distancing manoeuvre, indicating she wanted him out of her life.

Feeling thus abandoned and forsaken by both mum and dad had made Tony want to die, and he had attempted suicide in the hope that this would matter enough to his mother and father to bring them back together. As he noticed that it drove his mother even further away, he became more depressed.

Teresa was amazed that well-intentioned acts had had such a negative impact. She was also moved by the way in which Tony tried to help her to see how she had alienated her husband with similar attempts at leaving him free of her. At this stage, Teresa's counselling sessions began turning around her difficulty in acknowledging her need to love and be loved, and we uncovered her reluctance to let others know of her longings.

Her son's communication to her had broken the ice of her self-deception, and had penetrated through my therapeutic blindness and collusion with Teresa's presumptions about herself. How often do we carry on colluding with clients' negative beliefs about themselves and the world without an outspoken and rebellious, suffering teenager to point the way? I dread to think, and I am grateful for the quirks of life that show up the blind spots and culs-de-sac that I get caught up in.

Obviously my insight into what Teresa was doing wrong, once again, had its resonance in issues that were alive for me at that time in my relationship to my own children. I too had to learn that to give love as freely as one wishes, without reserve or fear of being abusive, is often kinder for the child than holding back with well-meaning, non-intrusive but stifled affection.

Being truthful about one's love also implies showing one's need for the other and sharing apprehensions and self-doubt. Although I had long learnt this to be crucial in adult relationships, I found it harder to be confident on this score with my children, assuming I had to protect them from confrontation with my human weaknesses. What I discovered was that it was preferable for them to have overt exposure to my limitations rather than being covertly condemned to them while labouring under the impression of my superiority.

My own learning coincided with Teresa's. This confirmed another growing conviction, namely that productive counselling work inevitably stretches the counsellor beyond habitual responses and patterns of living. Good counselling alters the counsellor's outlook as much as the client's, and until this process of mutual impact and reverberation has begun, the work remains superficial and glib.

Conclusion

In all of the situations I have described, what was needed most was to take a good hard look at what was actually present in front of me. It is remarkably difficult to take stock of a situation and genuinely see what is there. It is ridiculously easy to be led astray and soothed into the false and fatal belief that you understand, when actually, with all your experience and know-how, you are still engaged in thinking in patterns and applying formulae.

What comes out through all five instances is the sense of being bound by my personal circumstances. My learning is tied up with my private interests and personal preoccupations. While these shine a particular light on the client's issues, they often at first stand in the way of my understanding, especially when the client's struggles parallel my own, which seems to be predictably the case.

I now, mercifully, recognize this is not a tragic failing on my part, and it does not simply occur through lack of training or insufficiency of personal analysis: it happens inevitably because I am, beyond training and self-understanding, bound by the same existential dilemmas as my clients. It is a fact of life that we are never perfectly equipped to help others, and we are never exempt from the human condition in which we intervene.

I would go further and argue that it is precisely because we share the same human condition in all its contradictions and imperfections with our clients that we can be of assistance to them. We would become incapable of being of much help if we were not ourselves deeply engaged in the fight for survival. What a relief to renounce the striving for perfection once we realize how insufferable we would be if we could achieve true superiority, sainthood, or a state of total self-knowledge!

My experience illustrates only too clearly that it is just as dangerous to think yourself above and beyond your clients' troubles as it is to feel overwhelmed by them. In my examples I have illustrated both ends of the spectrum, and in each of these situations it was the client's distress or process that eventually pointed to a solution. The times when I came to the edge of my understanding were thus the very times that the clients' issues showed the way forward.

So let us be grateful for the clients who do not fit our formulae and patterns, the ones who fight us and make life difficult for us. Let us count our blessings for making mistakes, for these are the moments when we get thrown back into chaos and disarray, when we lose our foothold and are forced to stretch beyond already acquired knowledge and insight. For at the end of the day it is the error we remember, and the easy success merely soothes us to slumber and dream our grandiose dreams of professional excellence and glorious omniscience.

Learning comes from seeing what is wrong and what is lacking. One thing I have learnt for sure is that I shall forever be lacking. I have faith in my own failures as guidelines to my work, and because of this I can have similar faith in my clients' ability to learn from their mistakes. Instead of setting standards that neither they nor I can reach, the trick is to be fully committed to the opening up of the darkest recesses of experience. To let the light shine where darkness was is enough to keep on the right track and be challenged.

If we are to help clients to get a grip on the paradoxes that elude them, we must be prepared to be exposed to these paradoxes ourselves. In the process we will be subjected to continuous challenges and confronted with ever-new aspects of human experience. Relentless self-examination and reflection are required to deal with it and make sense of it, when it becomes apparent we do not yet grasp the full extent of our clients' difficulties. Together, with them, we must expect to be faced by new complications and mysteries, and we must be ready for a critical reconsideration of set ideas about life. To me it is this process of persistent reappraisal and questioning of what I am and how the world works that makes the counselling profession so fascinating. It would otherwise be a dull and depressing job.

Counselling is about being human with other human beings and allowing them to let their humanity unfold. If, as I believe, to be human means to err, we must have no compunction and false pride over erring, as long as we are willing to retrieve our steps and mend our ways as often as necessary.

I think that one of the things we need in counselling is more humility about our ignorance. Writing up some of my own mistakes and lessons learnt has shown me once more just how hard it is to have such humility publicly. It has been much easier in earlier publications (1984, 1988, 1990) to recount cases where I felt some pride in my performance. Yet there is a curious satisfaction in mentioning the failures and letting go of the professional bulwark of pride and dignity. Openly admitting how biased and limited one is, how faltering and bumbling one's attempts at understanding life is, to say the least, humbling. To do so and find peace with one's errors is strangely exhilarating. It is something I strongly recommend.

References

Barnes, M. and Berke, J. (1973) *Mary Barnes: Two Accounts of a Journey Through Madness*. Harmondsworth: Penguin.

Binswanger, L. (1962) *Being-in-the-World* (trans. J. Needleman). New York: Basic Books.

Boss, M. (1957) *Psychoanalysis and Daseinanalysis* (trans. J. B. Lefebre). New York: Basic Books.

Cooper, D. (1967) *Psychiatry and Anti-psychiatry*. New York: Barnes and Noble.

Deurzen-Smith, E. van (1984) 'Existential therapy', in W. Dryden (ed.), *Individual Therapy in Britain*. London: Harper and Row.

Deurzen-Smith, E. van (1988) *Existential Counselling in Practice*. London: Sage Publications.

Deurzen-Smith, E. van (1990) 'Existential therapy', in W. Dryden (ed.), *Individual Therapy: a Handbook*. Milton Keynes: Open Univ. Press.

Laing, R. D. (1960) *The Divided Self*. Harmondsworth: Penguin.

Laing, R. D. (1961) *Self and Others*. Harmondsworth: Penguin.

Laing, R. D. (1967) *The Politics of Experience*. Harmondsworth: Penguin.

4 Windy Dryden

I became interested in counselling as a direct result of pursuing a PhD in social psychology. My topic was self-disclosure, and many of the papers I was reading at that time concerned self-disclosure in counselling. These articles awakened a powerful response in me, and this, together with my experiences of going to encounter groups in the late 1960s and early 1970s, led me to conclude that I wanted to become a counsellor.

My first major training was a one-year, full-time diploma in counselling in educational settings at Aston University. This course was basically a training in client-centred counselling, with some emphasis on behavioural techniques for specific problems such as examination anxiety.

For reasons that will become apparent later in this chapter, I came to the conclusion that I needed further training, and enrolled on a two-year, part-time course in psychodynamic psychotherapy. This was an introductory course, and served to convince me that this approach was not for me. During it I developed an interest in rational-emotive therapy (RET) and decided to pursue further training in this approach. This I did part-time from 1977 to 1980 at the Institute for RET in New York. At about the same time I studied for an MSc in psychotherapy at Warwick University with John and Marcia Davis. This eclectic course helped me to integrate some of my previously disparate training and practical experiences, and underscored for me that developing and maintaining a productive working alliance is a crucial ingredient in effective counselling and psychotherapy.

Subsequent training in Aaron Beck's cognitive therapy in Philadelphia, and Arnold Lazarus's multimodal therapy in Princeton, New Jersey extended my practice as an eclectically orientated counsellor, albeit one who is firmly in the rational-emotive and cognitive-behavioural tradition.

My experience of working with clients has been quite broad. I have worked with individuals in a university counselling service, a GP practice, a clinic which specializes in helping clients who are depressed, and a clinical psychology department. I have worked with couples in Relate, and with groups at the Institute for RET as Albert Ellis's co-therapist. I don't work with families when there are children or adolescents involved, because I believe this work requires special skills which I do not have. As you can imagine, all this training and experience has provided me with many opportunities to learn the hard way.

Thriving on variety

In April 1981 I went to Philadelphia to begin a six-month sabbatical at the Center for Cognitive Therapy. My intention was to gain a thorough training, and to this end I resolved to restrict myself to clinical practice so that I was not distracted from my purpose.

It is important to stress at this point that I had always had variety in my working life. My first and, at this juncture, only job was as lecturer in counselling at Aston University. My duties there were quite varied, and involved training and supervising counselling trainees, counselling students at the university's counselling service, administration, and academic writing/research. I had never counselled full-time – something I regarded as a lacuna in my career to date, and one I was keen to fill. There was something amiss, I reasoned, when someone whose main job was to train people to work as full-time counsellors had never worked as a full-time counsellor himself. So I was doubly enthusiastic – first, about immersing myself in an exciting, new approach to counselling, and second, about working as a practitioner. I would take a break from writing and recharge my batteries by refraining from any involvement in training and supervising activities. After all, wasn't that partly what constituted a sabbatical – a break from one's usual duties?

After an initial intensive training in the fundamentals of cognitive therapy, I was deemed to be competent enough to see clients at the Center, and as I had about six years' experience as a counsellor, I was given a reasonably heavy load of about twenty cases. I set off with considerable enthusiasm. I enjoyed the cases I was assigned, and revelled in the expert, one-to-one supervision I received. 'This is the life', I thought, and the idea that I had been missing something fundamental by not working as a full-time counsellor strengthened in my mind.

Then it happened. I began to feel increasingly restless and irritable for no apparent reason. Initially, I couldn't understand what these feelings pointed to, so I decided to apply some of the cognitive techniques I had recently learned and had been applying with my clients on myself, in the hope that this would shed some light on my puzzling experience. In particular, I decided to investigate my automatic thoughts, that is, those thoughts that would pop into my head automatically without any conscious intent. Here is a simple sample of those thoughts and how I responded to them:

> I'm just not cut out to be a counsellor.
> *Response:* That's not true. I've been seeing clients now for over six years, and I've never questioned my suitability before. I'm doing reasonably well with the clients with whom I'm working, so I don't think it's true that I'm not cut out to be a counsellor.
>
> I'm not cut out to be a cognitive therapist.
> *Response:* Well, it's true that I have some doubts about cognitive therapy. In lots of ways, I favour RET, which, although similar to cognitive therapy in many respects, is quite different in others. However, I don't think this explains the full extent of my restlessness and irritability, which was now quite marked.
>
> There's something missing in my life.
> *Response:* Now that seems far closer to the heart of the matter. I know there's nothing amiss in my personal life. I've just got married and have my lovely wife with me, so that's not it. However, I do feel there's something missing in my work. What am I not doing that I'm used to and that I enjoy?

It was when I asked myself this last question that the mist began to clear. I missed the other activities that constituted the varied nature of my work at Aston University. It was the variety that I was missing! Once the issue had become clear, the remedy was simple. First, I began to plan an academic paper that compared and contrasted RET with cognitive therapy (1984). Then, I made arrangements to fulfil the trainer and supervisor parts of myself by travelling weekly to the Institute for RET in New York to participate in their training programmes, and serve as one of their supervisors. I did all this while maintaining the same caseload at the Center for Cognitive Therapy.

What this experience taught me was that I thrive on variety in my work, and when this missing, I very quickly become unfulfilled with consequent feelings of restlessness and irritability. It was a profound learning experience, albeit a difficult one, and I have taken heed of it ever since.

The importance of being an 'authentic chameleon'

In 1981, Arnold Lazarus published a book entitled *The Practice of Multimodal Therapy*, in which he introduced the concept of the counsellor as 'authentic chameleon'. By this he meant that it is important for counsellors to vary their interpersonal style with different clients, but in an authentic manner. In the same year, and well before I had read Lazarus's book, I learned the hard way about the value of being an 'authentic chameleon'.

At the time that I learned this lesson I was working at the Center for Cognitive Therapy. I was assigned Ian, a forty-two-year-old man who was quite depressed. Early on in counselling he spoke about his previous therapists, but in a pejorative fashion. He complained they were 'a bunch of stuffed shirts', who acted very formally towards him and who sat behind their desks. 'Their dress reflected their manner', he went on, saying that it was as if they wore white coats, such was the interpersonal distance between them and him. In response to my question concerning the type of therapeutic relationship he was seeking, he said he was looking for someone with whom he could loosen up and 'rap'. His preferred image was of the two of us sitting with our feet up on the coffee table discussing his problems in a very informal way, or 'shooting the breeze' as he put it.

Now, I saw no good reason why I could not practise cognitive therapy in this way, and so week after week we would have our 'rap' sessions, as Ian came to call them, while I conceptualized my approach as informal cognitive therapy. I followed all the strategic and technical rules of the therapy, but did so while using a lot of self-disclosure, within a relationship which looked for all intents and purposes as two friends having a heart-to-heart discussion about the problems of one of them. We did indeed take to putting our feet up on the coffee table, and what is more we took turns bringing to the session cans of soda, which we consumed during the therapy hour. The outcome was a salubrious one, and at the end of our work together Ian pointed to our friendly, informal relationship as the most important therapeutic factor, from his vantage point.

Three weeks after I started seeing Ian, I was assigned Mrs G, a fifty-seven-year-old woman who had a considerable problem with anger over what were a number of minor environmental stressors. At our first session, she told me she was looking forward to meeting me because she always found Englishmen very correct and civilized, and fully expected me to observe the protocol of a professional relationship, unlike her previous therapist, who, she claimed, was overly friendly and who she sacked 'in very short order'.

Now, it should be noted that I saw Mrs G an hour before my session with Ian, and it was this temporal proximity that made life difficult for me, but which provided me with the learning that has stayed with me ever since. Every counsellor, I believe, has an interpersonal style which is natural to him or her, and mine was closer to the informality I demonstrated with Ian than to the stark formality demanded by Mrs G; and when I use the term 'demanded' I do so advisedly. For Mrs G reprimanded me for every slip into what she considered to be an inappropriately informal relationship. Before I fully learned my lesson, I made what proved to be the following errors with Mrs G, each of which met with a sharp rebuke: first, I once used her first name, to which she replied, 'Dr Dryden, will you please refrain from calling me by my Christian name'; second, I once tried to illustrate a therapeutic point by making a disclosure about my own similar experience, to which Mrs G replied, 'Dr Dryden, I am not paying the Center good money to hear about your personal problems'; and, third, I once greeted her at the beginning of the session without my jacket and tie, wrongly thinking (or perhaps hoping!) that I was seeing Ian; her reply was, 'Dr Dryden, will you please put on your jacket and tie.' Once I had fully digested the point, namely that I had to be strictly formal with Mrs G, we got on famously, and she made quite good headway overcoming the problems for which she sought therapy.

What I learned starkly was that different clients benefit from different types of bonds with their counsellor, and that if we are going to take seriously the point that clients are different, we need to acknowledge that one way in which they differ concerns their expectations of what is a helpful counsellor style. Furthermore, I learned that as long as the counsellor has that style in his or her repertoire, and can be authentic in adopting the style – which, importantly, should not reinforce the client's problems – then there is much to be gained by being an 'authentic chameleon'.

Different strokes for different folks

I have been influenced by the work of Ed Bordin (1979), who has written sensitively about the working alliance in counselling and psychotherapy. He argues that there are three major components of the alliance which need to be considered when appraising our counselling work with clients. These components are bonds, i.e., the relationship between counsellor and client and its vicissitudes; goals, i.e., the objectives that counsellor and client have concerning their work together; and tasks, i.e., the activities in which counsellor and client engage in their quest to help the client achieve his or her goals.

In the previous section I discussed the lesson I learned in the bond domain of the alliance. In this section I will discuss a similar lesson I learned in the task domain. In fact, I had to learn the lesson several times before I grasped its true message.

As I mentioned, I was originally trained in client-centred counselling. I remember being very enthusiastic about this approach when I was learning about it, and considered that I had found the key to helping people. My first clients responded well to this approach, and this early experience tended to reinforce my unitary view of the counselling universe. Eventually, however, an increasing number of my clients indicated that they wanted more from counselling than the empathy, respect, and genuineness I was offering them. For a time I thought the fault lay with me. The reason I wasn't helping these clients, I thought, was because I wasn't being empathic, respectful, or genuine enough. This view was in fact reinforced in supervision as my supervisor and I pored over my counselling tapes, looking for instances of my inaccurate empathy.

I remember one case in particular when my client and I struggled for weeks until I broke ranks and, taking a leaf out of Albert Ellis's book, I successfully helped the client by strongly attacking her rigidly held belief that she needed approval in order to be happy. This case proved to be one of the influences that led me to go New York to train in RET.

Again I thought I had found the Holy Grail. It was clear to me that all clients held irrational beliefs, and therefore my task was clear – to help them to identify, challenge, and change these beliefs using a host of cognitive, emotive, and behavioural techniques. Indeed, I had a lot of success using RET. However, not all clients responded well to this approach.

So how did I initially deal with these expectations? I did what people tend to do when faced with potentially threatening information: I denied it, or I distorted it to protect my unitary view. So the client who kept claiming I was not listening to her closely enough was labelled, I hate to admit it now, a 'resistant client'; the man who wanted to talk at length about his childhood experiences at boarding school was given the standard RET line that it was his present beliefs about these experiences that were the real root of his problem, and if only he would change these then all would be well. A third example of my failure in the task domain of the alliance occurred early in my career when through lack of knowledge I omitted to employ a variant of response prevention with a client with a handwashing compulsion – a task which the research literature clearly demonstrates is indicated for this type of problem. In my naïvety, I once again thought that empathy, etc., was all-powerful.

It took quite a bit of disconfirming evidence to disabuse me of my unitary view of the counselling universe. I now believe that different clients need to perform different tasks in counselling at different points in the process. If this idea is correct, then I, as a counsellor, need to be proficient in a wide variety of counselling tasks myself, or refer the client to someone who is better equipped to help them – an issue I take up in my next hard-earned lesson.

Does this mean I am no longer a rational-emotive counsellor? Well, yes and no. I still use rational-emotive theory as a core theoretical framework; however, I am much broader in my use of counselling tasks than I used to be, and much more receptive to my clients' views of what will be of value to them in the counselling process. In short, I now have a pluralistic view of counselling rather than a unitary one.

I may not be the best person to help

In my early days as a counsellor, I fluctuated between thinking I had discovered the answer to all clients' problems, to feeling quite uncertain about my ability to help anyone. One way I compensated for the latter was to believe I had to take on anyone who came to me for help. The idea that I might not be the best person to counsel someone was so threatening that the thought rarely, if ever, entered my mind.

Fortunately, I had several experiences with clients that led me to revise this view. One example which stands out in my mind occurred when I lived and worked in Birmingham. I was fairly well known at that time for practising rational-emotive therapy, and in those days I was far less flexible in its practice than I think I am now.

One evening I received a call from a man who said he had been referred to me for what he called 'RT therapy'. Before rational-emotive therapy was known as 'RET' it was called 'rational therapy', or 'RT' for short. I remember thinking it was a bit odd for someone to call RET by its older abbreviation 'RT'; however, I did not pursue it over the phone, and we proceeded to make an appointment for an assessment session.

After telling me about his various problems, the man asked how I thought I could help him. I responded with a brief overview of RET, how his problems could be traced to a number of faulty beliefs and attitudes, and how we would work together to help him to identify, challenge, and change these beliefs. He listened patiently, but after I had finished he shook his head and said he hadn't heard such a load of intellectualized rubbish in a long time.

Apparently, the person who effected the referral mistook RET for Reichian therapy (RT), a body-orientated approach to therapy which is based on the idea that people's problems are related to energy blockages that are located in various parts of the body, and which require body-orientated interventions such as deep massage. These interventions will, according to the theory, help to free these blockages so that the person's psychic energy can be restored. As you may appreciate, this is a far cry from the theory and practice of RET, so instead of trying to disabuse the man of his ideas of what caused his problems and what he considered he needed to resolve them, I effected a further referral to a local therapist who I knew used Reichian techniques. I heard later that my referral yielded very positive results for the client. This experience led me to begin to question the unquestionable: perhaps I couldn't help everyone.

This tentatively held conclusion was strengthened as my name began to become more widely known in the counselling community. However, as this happened, increasingly I received calls from prospective female clients who either thought my name was 'Wendy' Dryden, or that Windy was a woman's name. A typical conversation would go like this:

Woman: Can I speak to Windy Dryden please?
Me: Speaking. How can I help you?
Woman: No, I'm sorry, you misheard me. I asked for Windy Dryden. She's a female counsellor.
Me: My name is Windy Dryden. I'm often mistaken for a woman because of my first name.
Woman: I'm sorry to trouble you, but I'm looking for a woman counsellor. 'Bye.

I have had this kind of conversation many times now. In fact, I have gained much firsthand experience of numerous women not wanting to see me for counselling because I am a man.

These and similar experiences have led me to conclude that I may well not be the best person to help a client. I am much more comfortable with this idea now, at a time when I am confident in my ability as a counsellor, than I was earlier in my career when I was more uncertain of this ability, and when I had more to prove to myself.

The consequences of realizing that I may not be the best person to help is that I now refer prospective clients to other counsellors a lot more than I used to. As Arnold Lazarus has put it (Dryden, 1991), one of our tasks in counselling is to know our own limitations and other counsellors' strengths. By all means we should work to minimize our limitations, but since we will always have our fallibilities as practitioners, it behoves us to refer clients to others who are better placed to help. I can now do this with satisfaction, whereas earlier in my career, if I did it at all, it was with a sense of failure.

'You didn't ask me!'

One of the most painful lessons I have had to learn as a counsellor is that sometimes I just don't seem to learn – that I seem to make the same mistakes over and over again. When I first discovered this, I thought it applied just to me, since I hadn't read about it in the counselling literature. However, the more I supervised counsellors' tapes, which gave me access to what counsellors actually did in their sessions, as opposed to what they said they did, the more I realized, with relief, that it applied to other people as well.

A vivid example of this stands out in my mind. As I have mentioned, in 1981 I spent a six-month sabbatical at the Center for Cognitive Therapy in Philadelphia. One of the clients I saw there was a forty-two-year-old housewife who was severely depressed. She had had psychoanalytic psychotherapy without any appreciable benefit, and was referred to the Center as it had a growing reputation for the treatment of depression.

The client, whom I will call Phyllis, responded very well to cognitive therapy, and in five months or so her score on the Beck Depression Inventory went from being in the severely depressed range to being in the non-depressed range. At the end of the therapy the client seemed happy with the outcome of our work together. I was also happy, and so was my supervisor. Now, one of the features of the therapy that accounted for its success, or so I thought, was the quality of our relationship. Phyllis and I seemed to get on rather well, and she had a good sense of humour, which I capitalized on during the therapy. At times this humour seemed to be what I called 'overly giggly', but I attributed this to the exuberance of Phyllis's personality. How wrong I was!

A year later I returned to the Center for a visit, and was encouraged to schedule a follow-up session with all the clients I had seen a year previously. Among these was Phyllis. When I met her, she seemed altogether more serious than when I had known her. She had maintained the gains she had made in therapy with me with respect to her depression, but mentioned, almost casually, that in the past year she had had treatment for 'my long-standing alcohol abuse problem'. 'What long-standing alcohol abuse problem? You didn't tell me you had an alcohol problem', I whined pitifully, or so it seems now, ten years later. 'Well,' she replied with more than a hint of irony in her voice, *'you didn't ask me!'*

As you can imagine, I didn't feel too good about this, which of course is an understatement. I felt wretched. My initial reaction was to write to the University of Aston, which employed me at that time, and tender my resignation. How could I possibly train counsellors if I could make such a ridiculous blunder? However, common sense prevailed, and instead I resolved to ask all my subsequent clients about their drinking and drug intake, which I did, or so I thought I did until the episode with Emily.

Emily was an artist who, among other concerns, spoke of feelings of emptiness. I had been working with her for about two years, during which she had begun to extricate herself from being trapped in her vocation by enrolling for a university course. She also had made reasonable progress in overcoming long-standing social and performance-related anxieties. However, we had arrived at an impasse, and Emily came to sessions with increasing anxiety, for which she offered no clear explanation. I realized something was amiss, but couldn't put my finger on what this was. Soon after, Emily came to a session in a state of extreme anxiety and handed me a letter to read. In it, Emily admitted that she had a long-standing drink problem, consuming regularly a bottle of wine a day. Dumbfounded, I again blurted out the question, 'Why haven't you told me before?' I saw my whole counselling life flash before my eyes as I processed her reply, which was, as you may have guessed, '*You didn't ask me!*'

I have several other examples where I mistakenly thought I had learned a lesson from counselling once and for all, but this is the most striking. Of course, there are several important questions to ask about my seeming lapse and, believe me, I have asked them both inside and outside supervision. The point I want to stress here is that as counsellors we don't learn something once and for all. We are human and subject to all the fallibilities this status endows. In counselling this may well mean we have our blind spots. For my own part, while I will of course resolve once again to ask all my clients about their drinking habits, I will be less horrified – but not less chastened – when some future client responds to my enquiry about their failures to disclose a secret drinking problem with the statement, '*You didn't ask me!*'

Conclusion

On re-reading these five hard-earned lessons, two major themes stand out: the importance of variety in counselling, and the inevitability of counsellor fallibility. The variety theme occurs in the first four lessons. In the first, I learned that I thrive on variety in my working life and that I would wilt, to some degree, if I ever had to work full-time as a counsellor for more than a short period of time. In lessons two and three, I learned that clients need a variety of responses from their counsellors in both the bond and task domains of the working counselling alliance. In lesson four I learned that if an individual counsellor has sufficient flexibility and authenticity to provide such varied responses to a broad range of clients, all is well and good; if not, then he or she should unashamedly refer them on to other practitioners who are more suitable.

The second theme concerns the fact that, being human, all counsellors have limitations. This theme is present in all five lessons. It appears in the first lesson in the guise of my own personal limitations concerning the composition of my working life. Apparently, I function much better in a work setting where there is scope for diversity. If I am to retain my enthusiasm for the field of counselling and to avoid burnout, then one way I can do this is to avoid a restricting range of work tasks. For some, working as a full-time practitioner provides sufficient variety, but not for me.

In lessons two and three I discussed the theme of counsellor limitations more implicitly. If different clients require a different kind of bond with their counsellors, even the most interpersonally flexible of counsellors will not be able to help everyone. Be as flexible as you authentically can, but know your interpersonal limitations is the message of lesson two, while a similar message, but with respect to the use of counselling tasks, is to be found in lesson three. The obvious conclusion in the light of the limitations of individual counsellors occurs in lesson four: don't hesitate to refer to other counsellors when you come up against your own limitations. Having limitations is inevitable, so you don't need to be ashamed of them is a message I would like to convey to beginning counsellors.

Although it is crucial for all counsellors to minimize their errors, the fifth and final lesson demonstrates that we may well come up against blind spots that defy mastery. It might be nice if we could eliminate all our blind spots, but maybe the consequent loss of our humanity would make us less helpful to our human clients. Perhaps that is the most helpful lesson of all.

References

Bordin, E. S. (1979) 'The generalizability of the psychoanalytic concept of the working alliance'. *Psychotherapy: Theory, Research and Practice*, 16, 252–60.

Dryden, W. (1984) 'Rational-emotive therapy and cognitive therapy: a critical comparison', in M. A. Reda and M. J. Mahoney (eds), *Cognitive Psychotherapies: Recent Developments in Theory, Research and Practice.* Cambridge, Massachusetts: Ballinger.

Dryden, W. (1991) *A Dialogue with Arnold Lazarus: 'It Depends'.* Milton Keynes: Open Univ. Press.

Lazarus, A. A. (1981) *The Practice of Multimodal Therapy.* New York: McGraw-Hill.

5 Michael Jacobs

I am one of those counsellors who would be hard pressed to convince any accreditation committee that I have had sufficient training. I have no formal qualifications, although a two-year, part-time course in psychoanalytic psychotherapy, personal therapy, and considerable supervision obviously stand me in good stead. I trained at a time when the philosophy – at least the psychoanalytic one – was still that you learned by experience, particularly personal therapy and supervision, and by the model the therapist and supervisor presented in person. I cannot underestimate the amount of learning that came from the sheer experience of being in a job where, as a student counsellor, I had not only to work with many clients, but with virtually any client who came. There was no one to select the right people for a beginner to see, or to take over the hard cases, although I was fortunate to have regular twice-weekly supervision from an experienced psychotherapist.

In the early 1970s, methods of teaching counselling with which we are now familiar, and, indeed, to which I have made a considerable contribution, were largely absent, at least in psychoanalytic training. Identifying, learning, and practising different constituent skills, or identifying issues in theory, and practising through role play different situations that may arise – none of this was there to teach and guide me. I literally learned the hard way. There must have been so many hard-earned lessons in the first few years as a full-time counsellor and therapist that, were I able to recall them all, it would be impossible to single out five. Fortunately, most of them have become integrated, without leaving obvious scars from the anxieties I often experienced.

Throughout my practical experience, the training I received, as well as my therapy and supervision, all had a strong influence on me. Much of what was said or written by my mentors was not only technically correct within the tradition of psychoanalytic therapy, but also, as far as I could judge, often fitted many situations I encountered; it made sense of much that clients told me.

But what no training can really do – although some courses or trainers might encourage it more than others – is to create an individual style. There is much that can be taught; there is much that is also caught; but in the end we all have to learn that each meeting of therapist and client is unique, and that no one can tell us exactly what to do, how to respond, or what to avoid. I have been especially aware of this as a trainer, supervisor, and writer when I find my teaching quoted back at me. There are times when I long to say, 'That's not the only way of doing it. I don't think I want to be taken as literally as that!'

What I have learned from experience as a therapist of twenty years, as a supervisor and trainer over some thirteen years, and as a writer of substance over ten years, is to see each session – whether counselling, supervision, or training – as an opportunity to be creative and to learn something new.

My five hard-earned lessons illustrate this process. The first four need to be seen as pairs of lessons, and in the juxtaposition of each pair there is a deliberate contradictory message. This contradictory factor leads directly to the fifth of my hard-earned lessons, one which summarizes, synthesizes, and represents what I have come to find most creative in my work.

It is creative to say and do nothing

Counselling skills training stresses the importance of the correct response: whether it is accuracy, empathy, or open and closed questions, counsellors learn the value of reacting appropriately. In psychodynamic technique in particular, much stress can be laid on the value of accurate interpretations. The ability to stay quiet and to tolerate silence is also taught as an indispensable part of the skill of listening: it is assumed that a therapist's silence is deliberate, and that it serves a definite purpose. Silence may be appropriate at particular points to facilitate the client.

What is much more difficult to learn, and probably can only be learned through hard experience, is that it can be all right to be quiet for different reasons, when lost for words, with no idea how to respond, and no clue as to what is happening. It is all right for skills to disappear. And it is not just acceptable for a counsellor to experience this sense of being lost for words or understanding: it may also be beneficial for the client to know that the counsellor feels this. Not only is it necessary for a counsellor to learn that he or she does not have all the answers; it is important for the client to experience that too, and I mean to *experience*, not just to *know* intellectually.

I have already told the following story in my first book (1982), but it stays with me, and must therefore have been an important lesson for me. I will own that it was me as a counsellor, not some fictitious curate, who once had a client who was generally depressed, and who on one occasion started by expressing the deepest despair and thoughts of suicide. I still remember how hopeless and helpless I felt throughout that session.

Although I was in those days meticulous in writing up my notes afterwards, I could not remember much of what she said: a sure indication that I had been preoccupied with my feelings, and not with hers. My feelings were partly of anxiety about her hold on life, and partly about my inability to say anything that felt remotely appropriate. When it came to the end of the session, I had uttered little, certainly nothing I thought of value. As she prepared to leave, I simply said I did not feel I had been very helpful, but we would meet again next week, and perhaps we would understand it better then. I am not sure whether I was thinking, 'Hope! hope!', or whether I was really unsure whether I would see her again for that to be put to the test.

I remained in my room for some time, although normally I would have gone out for lunch. After a long time sitting in something of the despair which my client probably also felt, I decided to snatch something to eat, and went outside. On my way across the campus, I ran into one of the university chaplains, a cheerful man for whom life was often a joke; I listened while he laughed his way through one of his own stories. Politely, I joined in the laughter, although I scarcely felt in the mood.

All that week I worried about my client, expecting at any time to have a phone call to say she had been admitted to hospital, or worse. I dreaded the next session, since I felt I had almost made a promise that I would by then understand what was troubling her, although I was not convinced she would be present.

The time for her session came. She arrived, wearing not her usual dark clothes, but bright colours, including a red head-scarf. She smiled as she sat down, and I could see she felt much better. She spoke about last week, and how she had wondered whether *I* would survive! She explained how relieved she had felt to see me talking to someone outside the Students' Union building, and to see me laughing, because she then had been convinced she had not caused me any harm.

I cannot claim that this one occasion alone changed me, although it had a profound impact on my faith in people to survive. But I have over a period of time become much more comfortable with feelings of helplessness, and with sharing them – when it has been appropriate – with a client. If I am confused, I will often say so; and if I do not understand, I will make it clear that as yet I do not know what it is about, especially if pressed for an answer. I even have found myself saying with considerable ease that it was right to do so, to a client who questioned whether we would ever know what caused a certain behaviour pattern in him, that it was possible we would never discover it, although it was something worth going on looking for.

It is creative to say what you think or feel

One of the cardinal rules which Freud suggested is that the therapist should match the client's free association with 'free-flowing attention'. This means that a counsellor must allow his or her mind to wander with the client's story, and to wonder about the different phrases the client uses. Such thoughts and feelings may tell the counsellor about the effect the client has on other people's feelings; about feelings or ideas which the client is experiencing; or about the counsellor's own digestive processes at work!

I regard this as fundamental to the process of counselling. It is indeed taught as part of the psychodynamic approach, frequently linked with counter-transference in its more positive sense. But what should the counsellor do with the feelings and thoughts that 'bubble up'? I was taught to wait to see whether the client provides confirmation of such thoughts, in which case a more accurate interpretation might be made; or that such feelings are a clue to understanding what the client is experiencing. Sharing feelings may be appropriate as an expression of empathy; but the counsellor's random, even obtrusive, thoughts are normally reckoned to be reserved for the counsellor's internal process of trying to understand, at the time and later in supervision.

And what happens when the counsellor is just plain bored? Some of my most difficult times have not been when the client is expressing strange or wild ideas and feelings, but when the client rambles on, monotonously preoccupied with self or with the details of the week, without any real expression of feeling and with no evidence of insight. These are hard times: client and counsellor become locked in a mutual unwillingness to break out of the prison of safe innocuousness; neither wishes to challenge the other. These are often the clients you really do not look forward to seeing.

The lesson I have learned from such clients is that it is creative to give expression to some of the 'ridiculous' words and phrases that float in and out of my consciousness like patches of blue sky on an otherwise overcast day. I was going to write, 'to give expression *at the appropriate time*', but such a phrase destroys the essential point I am making. The hard lesson is to give up waiting for the client to take the lead. Instead, provide the opening; voice what seems inappropriate, 'out of the blue'. We may fear losing the client, but there is often a breakthrough.

What is 'hard-earned' about this lesson is that although boredom is hard, it takes a long time to learn not to put up with it. And even when your hunch pays off, the lesson has to be learnt yet again, another time, sometimes even with the same client. The risk is that speaking out of the blue will be disastrous, although the most likely negative response is incomprehension, and nothing worse than that (especially with the client who is obsessionally bound up in self). It is a lesson that has been reinforced time and again for me in supervising counsellors, even when I am not bored, where expressing my hunch stands less chance of misleading or damaging than it might with clients. Now that I am learning that it is also appropriate in therapy too, I apply this lesson more and more with individual clients and in groups.

An early occasion of boredom stays with me. This client valued counselling, attending regularly and speaking freely. But I found myself incredibly sleepy listening to her. I thought at first it was the time of day: the last session on a Friday. Changing to a morning did not prevent my stifled yawns. I was forced in the end to acknowledge that I did not find my client's story interesting. I was really bored. Being unable to play with anything else, I played with words: one kept coming to mind: 'sex!'. What else would you expect of a Freudian? I pushed it away, trying hard to concentrate upon my client. But the word 'sex' came back. Eventually I interrupted and explained that I was finding my thoughts drifting, and I wondered whether this meant that she was herself avoiding something? I wondered, 'Could it be sex that you find difficult to talk about?'

It was indeed a difficult subject for her, and my broaching it helped. She was almost visibly released to talk about her sexual feelings and her relationships with men, all of which her parents had made her feel were 'not quite nice'. At this distance I realize I hardly said anything mind-blowing. But the lesson at the time was that I could have expressed my hunch a lot earlier. Waiting for confirmation, as I had often been taught was necessary, might have meant waiting for ever.

My group example is a little different. I was not bored, but I did feel uncomfortably out of step with the excitement and joy which seven members were expressing to an eighth, who had just had apparently good news. It felt hard not to share what the group was feeling, and what this one person was apparently experiencing. It felt even harder to dare to express my difference. I held back from doing so, thinking it was me who had a problem: perhaps I was envious, or just plain morose? It was the last meeting of the group before a break, so I also felt that even if I was right, I should not spoil the fun, or say anything which I could not pick up for a while. But I had by then learnt not to ignore a hunch. I gently but confidently said that it was difficult to interrupt when the group was so enthusiastic, but I thought that this one member might be feeling apprehensive, and because people here and elsewhere expected him to be so pleased, he might feel very lonely too (just as I did, although I did not add that). I was right. Tears followed, and later he thanked me for saying what I did.

It is creative to break the rules

My second pair of lessons might have been given a subtitle representing a similar polarity about the relationship between what a counsellor thinks and what his or her supervisor says.

I should make it clear that there are some aspects of counselling practice which are so obviously right or wrong that they do not enter into consideration in this pair of lessons about attitudes to rules: and one of the functions of a supervisor is obviously to check that these rules are observed. Such rules are nearly always reinforced by a code of ethics, and are not those which I question here: physical contact with sexual connotations, for instance, is one of those rules which I regard as inviolable, however apparently pure the motives of the counsellor. Confidentiality is another practically inescapable obligation. Exploitation of the client is a third.

There are other rules, which are normally equally carefully adhered to, which do not appear to have the same ethical dimension to them, but which a counsellor needs to learn how to implement. They are often to do with boundaries of time, but may involve other boundaries of role. Here again, while a supervisor is a check on bad practice, he or she also represents a bench-mark of what is assumed to be good practice. The supervisor in part embodies the tradition in which the counsellor is working. He or she is a representative of 'the rules'. What happens when the counsellor and the supervisor (or 'the rules') disagree, especially when issues of good practice are at stake?

As a counsellor I have learned to listen to myself as well as my client. I may find my thoughts and feelings telling me something about the client which the client is unable to tell me. In presenting a client in supervision I also need to listen to what my supervisor says, because my supervisor too may be telling me something which neither I nor my client are able to. While it is often the case that my supervisor knows more about therapy than I do, he or she and I know different things about the client.

Problems arise when the supervisor appears to be right, because what he or she says fits in with general standards of good practice and with apparently sound theory, but the advice conflicts with what the counsellor is experiencing. What happens when the client suggests one thing, and the supervisor (or 'the rules') suggests another? Or when the counsellor finds him or herself as 'piggy in the middle'? Perhaps the situation is made even worse when the counsellor finds that the supervisor's voice represents one half of what the counsellor is thinking, and the client's voice represents the other half. On whose side does the counsellor come down, and to which inner voice does the counsellor listen?

There are no clear answers, although my hard-earned lesson illustrates such a dilemma. It was the first real occasion when I recognized that it might sometimes be better to listen to myself, and not to my supervisor or 'the rules', however sound they may be. I do not know whether the outcome would have been different had I listened more to myself. What I do know is that the episode helped me to recognize the issues involved, and I hope now makes me a supervisor who is sympathetic to such potential difficulties.

It was the last session before the Christmas break. At its end my client gave me a wrapped present, which I opened later: it was a book with a title that might have been significant about her. My supervisor observed what the gift might mean, and what message the title might be trying to convey to me. She advised giving the book back, since it was neither right to accept gifts during therapy, nor would keeping it help the client to express her feelings more openly to me. Both reasons were convincing, although I also felt that the client would be very hurt if I returned her gift. I was torn between following my supervisor's advice – and my internalized technical rules, which I knew had some justification – and my concern about causing offence to my client. I did not want the book, and by this time would have preferred to give it away – it felt like dynamite! Indeed it was.

When I gave it back, I learned that I should have trusted my judgement. I could have used my supervisor's interpretations at the right point without returning the book. As it was, after the initial explosion, therapy resumed, and the manipulative aspects of my client, which my supervisor had pointed to, became more and more obvious. While I do not blame my supervisor, who was technically correct, and who did not insist I do as she recommended, what I learned was the need to believe my own assessment, and, even more important, to consider bending such 'rules' when it seems correct for the client.

It is creative to stick to the rules

The other side is that, particularly in the early days of my practice, I valued the definite suggestions which this same supervisor made, especially when I was unsure how to proceed. A good supervisor contains a counsellor's anxiety, arising over a difficult client, or at a time of real crisis. A good supervisor also knows when to go further than containing, by being pro-active in defending the counsellor against clients who abuse the therapeutic milieu. Sometimes it is right for a supervisor to give definite advice, or to impart a strong message which almost insists that the counsellor should act in a particular way to deal with a critical situation. Of course, a supervisor does not impose sanctions if the counsellor chooses not to follow such advice, or if the therapist finds it impossible, for one reason or another, to take the desired action. Only very rarely will a supervisor have to blow the whistle, although it is not these situations I have in mind.

The hard-earned lesson I recall here is about client behaviour which is unacceptable, and which breaks the conventions of therapy. The following examples remind me how beneficial it can be, for the client as well as the therapist, to enforce 'the rules'. They confirm how important it can be for supervisors or colleagues to exert the right kind of pressure on the therapist to do so.

A colleague whom I had supervised for several years was experiencing difficulties with a client. Her client did not want to leave at the end of a session, and persistently flung her arms around her counsellor. We got nowhere with attempts to understand what this clinging behaviour might be about. Neither could the right interventions be found. It felt impossible to prevent it happening by any other means than being straight down the line. I realized that it was difficult for the counsellor to act: she was almost sucked into responding sympathetically. Her therapist stance was lost in a nurturing parent response. I had to strengthen her therapist role. I insisted she tell her client firmly that she was not to move out of the chair or hold on to her, and to make sure she herself moved physically if necessary. Similarly, I underlined that the counsellor had to enforce the end of the session, however angry or rejected this might make the client feel. It was a struggle, but the boundaries were eventually re-imposed.

Some years later, I was talking to this same colleague about my own frustrations with a client who kept ringing me out of hours, and who was constantly asking for changes of time. I had successfully resisted these attempts to invade my private space or to alter my working schedule, but this did not stop my client's persistent efforts. The ongoing battle was getting me down. My colleague reminded me that I had been very firm with her on observing boundaries; she added that the time had come for me to be equally resolute against this invasion of my time. She told me very firmly that I had to start the next session by making it clear that I was not going to be misused.

I felt reluctant to start the next session in such a way, preferring a 'softly, softly' approach, which would involve waiting for the right moment to interpret my client's behaviour, which in theory made sense. This is probably what I would have settled for, had not my colleague, immediately prior to the start of my session, insisted once more that I had to act decisively. Had it been possible, she would have come in and stood over me while I said it! Her advice worked. It was not the end of the battle: but it was the end of that particular means of abusing me. In the process it re-established my therapeutic skill with this client.

In a group in which I was one of two therapists, we had one member who could be very forthright, frightening everyone into submission, including her therapists. Her behaviour could be destructive, and we were concerned lest she damage new members. My co-therapist said we should tackle her: it was quite clear that the good of the group came before the good of one member. I felt uneasy lest we lose her. In the end, the issue was forced on us and my co-therapist was proved right. Having lost two new group members as a result of her destructive attitude, we tackled her, much to the relief of the group; she metaphorically kicked and screamed, but we did not lose her, and it was indeed a point of major breakthrough. This also helped me to recognize that a counsellor cannot ignore, nor simply interpret, behaviour which flouts the usual conventions, and which knowingly or not abuses the counsellor's normal tolerance and acceptance. Standing firm, which often includes speaking out against such behaviour, is vital for the counsellor's ability to function as a therapist; and more often than not is a relief to the client.

It is right to be wrong – or it is wrong to be right

My final lesson, like the others, was not learned through a single episode, although I cite one example. This lesson encapsulates my reasons for juxtaposing my first four lessons in pairs. It is that two and two seldom make four. It is that I have in the end to accept that it is all right to be wrong, even when you are right, and all right to be right, even when you are wrong. Accepting this frees both the counsellor and the client for more creative work together.

My example has to be of the client whom I wrote up as a success story, after what seemed a very neat piece of time-limited, well-focused therapy. He appears in one of my books, and, after the book was published, this client returned, still experiencing difficulties. His return made me aware that I had not, after all, done such a neat job, and that my published success story was misleading. How many of my other clients, had they the opportunity to return, might make me feel the same shaking of my confidence in what I had done? On the other hand, my client returned because, so he said, it had been valuable the first time, and perhaps I could console myself that this was at least a slightly different problem. So we met for a longer time; and once more there was a sense of what he (or we?) had achieved, but this time more real because we had been together longer. The successful case in print could in some sense still stand.

And so it might have stayed, until eight years later another therapist approached me: 'I've just taken on Mr Y. He tells me he once saw you . . .' On the one hand, I was uncertain whether the comment was friendly information or was tinged with a slight feeling of triumph that I had been found out! On the other hand, I console myself with the remark of another ex-client, for whom I thought I had done little. Years later, she told me that seeing me had saved her life. The lesson is clear: you never know, especially at the time, when you have got it right or when you have got it wrong. There are too many variables, and too many other factors to be able to control outcome. Things do not often add up to the answer you think you have, or to the answer you want.

This lesson does not mean that therapists can afford to be careless or unconcerned. Each session remains as hard, or sometimes as straightforward, as before. It is important for me to let it go when the client leaves the room, either at the end of the session, or at the end of the contract. There is no more that I can do. I *will* worry, I *will* think about some clients more than others, and some will remain with me for life: but I must not imagine that worrying will make things better or worse: the only possible benefit is that some thoughts between sessions, including in supervision, may provide avenues of approach that might be worth trying. Even these thoughts have to bubble up; they cannot be forced into consciousness.

Much of this has been similarly confirmed for me by the experience of being a supervisor and also a writer. It is important to work well; but at the end of the counselling session, or at the end of a supervision session, or on completing a book, I have to let the client, the supervisee, or the book go, and trust them to find their own way in their own worlds. If in some sense they were once 'mine', they are no longer. There will be points that I forgot to make, or aspects that I did not see, mistakes that I did not recognize, and insights that have yet to come.

Conclusion

It is a cruel fiction not just to believe but even to hope that everything must go well, that everything should end neatly, or that clients should feel better now or for all time. Freud, the pioneering spirit in these enigmatic areas (to whom I find myself returning time and again), urged against 'therapeutic ambition'. He held out no more hope than that 'hysterical misery' could be transformed into 'common unhappiness'. If his philosophy is not mere pessimism, but is pragmatic realism, such a view provides the possibility of helping me to become a more relaxed counsellor than I was in the beginning, neither pressured by my clients nor by what pressures them, and not on the whole troubled by my clients between sessions.

If that seems cold and callous, I can only assure the reader that it is not, and this sense of being able to hold in, hold on and hold up communicates itself to the client as well. Occasionally and inevitably, to the few, often the most demanding, it seems that I am not doing enough, or caring enough: but with many clients such an attitude eventually releases them sufficiently from anxiety about what will happen in the future to be creative in the present.

Counselling and therapy have become a growth industry, and I am one of those who have benefited from it. There is a great danger that therapists will over-reach themselves in their desire to help, will make ambitious claims for their methods, and will bolster beliefs in their philosophy, all of which are partly, if not wholly, an illusion. Those who benefit from the lessons of pioneers may learn much from them. But what they are less likely to learn from them – because it was part of the *process* of discovery, rather than the *content* of it – is the value of uncertainty, aloneness, and doubt. Perhaps it is not a lesson that can be taught, but only an exhortation that can be made, always to leave plenty of room for contradictions and for everything that does not add up.

References

Jacobs, M. (1982) *Still Small Voice*. London: SPCK.

6   Dave Mearns

I find counselling to be too demanding a task for full-time working. Throughout most of my twenty years' counselling experience
it has been a part-time activity, set alongside training, supervision,
and research.

Most of my counselling experience has been in three contexts:
student counselling, private practice, and work with traumatized
war veterans. The psychological damage created by war can be
both acute and chronic, requiring great commitment in daily
counselling contracts with the patients. However, I find private
practice work to be even more personally demanding, partly due to
the broad range of clientele, but also for the continuous self-
evaluation occasioned by the fact that the client is paying
personally at the end of each session.

I suppose my training began with my degree in psychology,
although psychology is not a very good background for later training in counselling. While psychology is officially the study of
individual differences, its inevitable emphasis is on similarities
rather than differences between individuals. During my own person-
centred therapy training as visiting fellow to the Center for Studies
of the Person in 1972–3, much time was spent ditching psychological
ways of thinking about generalities of human behaviour. Instead,
we sought to regard the client as a unique individual, whose
experience of the world could not be predicted by psychological
theory. In any case, psychology has long ago lost its way in terms
of understanding the human experience: it concentrates on cognitive
functioning, while almost totally neglecting emotionality.

My approach to counselling is person-centred, with a spattering
of concepts from transactional analysis (TA). I think TA has some
beautiful concepts, but appears to be bereft of a theory of therapy.
One of my greatest delights as a person-centred practitioner is to
see the growth in the last decade of specialist training courses in the
UK. Before that time, students were introduced to the person-
centred approach by trainers who themselves had not received
specialized training. This tended to perpetuate a British myth of the
superficiality of the person-centred approach. Thankfully, the
thoroughly trained professionals, graduating from courses such as
PCAI (London), PCT (Britain) and soon from our own courses in
Jordanhill College, will be equipping Britain with specialists in the
approach.

In the person-centred approach, no distinction is drawn between counselling and psychotherapy. Indeed, more often the term 'person-centred therapy' is used. Whatever label is adopted, the person-centred practitioner is expected to be able to work at great depth within both the affective and cognitive realms of the client's experience, and to use his, the practitioner's, *self* fully in that work. Such working makes great demands of training and self-development. In this regard I have long been a strong supporter of the British Association for Counselling, which to date has maintained high standards of training, supervision, and practice, despite pressure from those who regard counselling as a largely amateur activity requiring only introductory training.

The invitation to describe five hard-earned lessons in counselling is a challenge in openness. How frank can I be? Will I avoid worrying too much about being understood? Will I choose the really difficult bits? Hopefully I can do all of this, and reflect the effort of this series of books to represent counselling in action – warts and all!

On not making assumptions about my client

One of the paradoxes of counselling is that consistently working at such depth with people teaches us an enormous amount about human experiencing, and yet that very learning can lead us to make inaccurate assumptions about individual clients. Once made, these assumptions take on a life of their own: we can even rationalize our client's denials in terms of *his* lack of self-awareness.

The following extract from a review meeting with the client Trudy embarrassingly illustrates the contortions I performed in an effort to hold on to my assumptions about her. The context of this review was as part of my research into the client's experience of counselling, but it proved too embarrassing to use in that earlier book in the series (Mearns and Dryden, 1990). For the purposes of that research, Trudy had accepted my invitation to discuss our experience of counselling two years previously. The following verbatim extract from the tape recording of our meeting needs no commentary:

> *Trudy:* I knew what I was doing, but you seemed confused most of the time.
> *Dave:* Yes, I think I *was* confused much of the time.
> *Trudy:* You kept probing my feelings, and I kept them out of things.
> *Dave:* Why did you keep your feelings out?
> *Trudy:* Because it was difficult enough to manage a separation from George (her husband) without being paralysed by a lot of feelings. I

know myself quite well. When I get into sad feelings I just stay there for ages, and things go from bad to worse.

Dave: I see . . . I kept thinking that you were avoiding your feelings.

Trudy: And you were right.

Dave: I guess I didn't accept that avoiding feelings was the best way to go about it.

Trudy: It was the best way for me – maybe not for other people – but I know me best.

Dave: I got caught up in all sorts of assumptions about you. For instance, you seemed so stuck for a while, and also you were avoiding feelings, that I began to link the two and pushed for your feelings.

Trudy: And I had to resist your pushing by staying stuck. Your pushing was a nuisance. I found myself procrastinating: you know, talking about changing without actually doing it. Like I got into a thing of wanting to change for you rather than for me. Of course that never worked. I kept on jumping back to where I was stuck.

Dave: I'm beginning to think that I didn't understand you at all during our time together.

Trudy: Yes, but I still got a lot out of it.

Dave: That was another thing I didn't understand. You suddenly decided to stop and yet you were quite clear that you had got a lot out of it. Frankly, I couldn't really see what you had got out of it. I even wondered if your stopping was what we call a "flight into health" – where the client suddenly gets better as a way of terminating the contact with the dreadful counsellor!

Trudy: Yes, in that last session you sounded suspicious; the way you kept going over and over things.

Dave: I suppose it was the only way I could make sense of it.

Trudy: You couldn't see how the time had been important for me?

Dave: No, I couldn't.

Trudy: Well, despite cul-de-sacs offered up by your repeated theories about how people in my position should feel and behave, the counselling sessions gave me time to go over and over and over things. Sometimes I need to go over the same thing a dozen times before I can let it go. A second reason was that I was able to compartmentalize the problem and my confusion about it. I could attend to it during our twice-weekly sessions, and to some extent leave it aside during the rest of the week. That helped me get by the initial months without falling into the kind of pit of despair, which is a real trap for me.

Dave: So the time was helpful – *despite* me?

Trudy: *Very* helpful.

Dave: I can't get over how many wrong assumptions I made about you: even at the beginning of our time together I didn't trust the unrestrained relief you expressed about the separation. I presumed that this was masking something else that you were blocking out.

Trudy: Listen, if I were to summarize my feelings about George walking out on me it would be 65% relief, 30% sadness, and 5% assorted other feelings. Getting stuck in the sadness bit would not have been an honest reflection of me, never mind the fact that it would have stopped everything else.

Dave: I guess I'm still harbouring the theory that avoiding feelings is a short-term policy.

Trudy: Now you're in danger of getting some angry feeling from me – and I don't mind expressing anger! Can't you see that I don't fit your theories? If you really understood what I mean by my despair you would know how pointless it is for me to go there.

Dave: Even when you ended our sessions, I rationalized it with the assumption that 'you hadn't really been ready for counselling'.

Trudy: You guys can really tie things up neatly with your theories. Pity you don't know what's really in the parcel!

Trudy was a very patient teacher during that interview. As her pupil, the lesson for me was all the harder because I had 'learned' it many times before. The lesson is that while my previous experience and learning may help me to feel clever, it tells me absolutely nothing about my new client. Furthermore, my need to feel clever may detract from my work with that client.

On the self-concept striking back

If my excessive theorizing had a deleterious effect on my work with Trudy, there were also numerous clients who have suffered from my lack of theoretical understanding of the roller-coaster that is the therapeutic process. These were clients with whom the work had been progressing particularly well, until suddenly and inexplicably they seemed to become completely stuck, or even to regress.

One example was Scott, a man who was prominent and effective in the business community, but almost totally inadequate in interpersonal relationships, particularly where emotions were involved. During the first six months of our work, Scott developed considerable understanding of his self and of his self-in-relationship at work, with his wife, and with his children. Scott was a man who used his brain most effectively, and this was exemplified in the counselling room. His way into the whole process was to develop a cognitive understanding of his emotions. His understanding eventually extended to his own history, and what he came to recognize as the emotional abuse he had suffered from his father.

During that first six months, Scott showed nothing which resembled a feeling: neither joy, sadness, or anger. However, in the seventh month, Scott's affect started to loosen. He began to see that he could be a different person from the way he had come to see himself. In his communication with his wife, Scott began to express his feelings: sadness, regret, and tentative, loving feelings. In relation to one of his employees, he communicated uncharacteristic empathy, and with his children he found himself more able to play.

Just as quickly as Scott's changing manifested itself in his behaviour, the process stopped, and indeed reversed. Within a few weeks, Scott was thoroughly cut off from other people and had begun drinking heavily. He missed three consecutive appointments without making prior contact. When I telephoned him after the third missed appointment, he referred to the fact that he was 'too far gone to really change', and said he wanted to stop our sessions. His voice was cold and detached; indeed, I found myself feeling a little threatened by his detachment, as if I was imposing in an unwanted way. I muttered something about being available any time he wanted to take things up again, and then I let him go.

I only realized my mistake with Scott and others like him some years later when changed circumstances, and perhaps my greater self-confidence, led me to hold on in this kind of situation. I found that holding on led to dramatic movement on the part of some clients.

Although I have given psychology rather a bad press at the beginning of this chapter, I find it helpful in understanding this aspect of the therapeutic process; in particular, dissonance theory seems to provide an economical description of what is happening for a client like Scott. The process of counselling or therapy creates dissonance within the self-concept. 'Dissonance' is a psychological term denoting the experience of an inconsistency, which creates tension. For Scott, the inconsistencies which developed centred on his awakening emotionality. He regarded himself as a 'cold, unemotional, consistent person' (his words in our third meeting). Yet, in the last weeks of his work in counselling, he had seen himself express love, hate, anger, and deep sadness. These emotions had extended to his outside life, thus offering powerful inconsistency with his self-concept.

There are two main ways in which such dissonance might have been reduced. One possibility is that Scott would continue his changing in the direction of self-acceptance and consequent self-concept change. When clients make this choice they usually experience it as irreversible: there is no way back to the old self. The other possibility at this critical point is that the self-concept strikes back. If the latter process becomes established and goes unchallenged, then the dissonance is reduced in such a way as preserves the self-concept at the expense of the therapy. In a sense I colluded with that part of Scott's personality which fought to retain the old self-concept. I was over-awed by the strength and detachment of that part. Had I functioned in a more effective therapeutic way, I would have acknowledged that part of his personality, but also sought out the other parts. Instead, I colluded with one subpersonality (Rowan, 1990), and we ended the counselling.

The lesson in this for me is that the therapeutic process is much more complex than I am inclined to assume. The road towards progress can have sidings and reverse loops; I must be patient and strong in that varied process lest, as in the case of Scott, I grab failure from the jaws of success.

On sufficiency and commitment

Most of the counselling or therapy offered in mental health contexts in our culture does not offer sufficient help for the severely troubled patient or client to take the risks which would be necessary for movement. Such help is offered in units and frequencies which offer convenience to the helpers with scant regard to the needs of the clientele. The ultimate irony is that those patients for whom the proffered help is insufficient are labelled 'inappropriate for counselling/psychotherapy'. This mechanism of blaming the victim is a standard way for an institutionalized social system to protect its boundaries.

In my experience, counselling is an incredibly powerful dynamic if it is occurring in a context which is sufficient for the needs of the client. Within my own person-centred approach, reference is frequently made to the three basic conditions of empathy, unconditional positive regard, and congruence. I find it helpful to think in terms of the necessity of a fourth condition, namely that the therapeutic context be sufficient for the needs of the client. Were this a theoretical treatise, we could go on to define the constituents of sufficiency in terms of length of sessions, frequency, the physical context, but also the fullness of the counsellor's commitment as experienced by the client.

The hard-earned lesson for me has to do with this notion of commitment. Certainly, the hysterical, mute, war-damaged client would be inappropriate for a counselling context which offered only one hour per week in a fancy office, or even daily hospital group therapy as that is conventionally conceived in its now-sanitized form. However, my experience is that the offer of a lengthy commitment to individual work for one hour per day, seven days a week, in a holding hospital environment can be sufficient. In a way, the problem of commitment becomes one of offering a sufficiency of context which is larger than the size of the prison the client has built around himself.

As the profession of counselling becomes more in danger of institutionalization, its protective mechanisms seek to punish deviants. Either the client is blamed in terms of his inappropriateness for counselling, or the counsellor who would offer a huge commitment is accused of the crime of over-involvement. The notion of counsellor over-involvement offers a ready sanction to apply to the deviant counsellor who wishes to offer more than the inadequate norm with respect to therapeutic context.

Perhaps the label of 'over-involvement' would be applied to me in my work with Bill, a bereaved client who had lost his wife and two of his children in a car accident. For a number of weeks I tried to work with Bill twice weekly in his own home. It was necessary to work in his home because he carried an understandable fear of leaving his one remaining child. In almost every session we would reach the edge of his despair and he would pull back. As he said, 'If I go further into this I might not be there for Sally [his remaining child] in the morning.'

The therapeutic context we had created was not sufficient for Bill's needs. The way we solved the problem was borrowed from one of my early mentors, André Auw. Instead of continuing with an ineffective pattern, we set a week aside some months in advance. For that week we arranged the hire of a country cottage, and Bill found it possible to put Sally in the care of his mother. Needless to say, the pace of the therapeutic process during those seven days was dramatic. The context allowed us to meet in a variety of ways, all of which tended to enhance trust. As well as working together, we cooked meals, washed up, went for walks, did some fishing, and even repaired a leaky roof together. Also, the flexible structure enabled some very lengthy sessions, including one of ten hours on the fourth day. I doubt whether Bill could have faced the question of his suicide in any other therapeutic context. He had to be free from the rest of his life to face that question for himself alone. So often the contexts in which we work with people do not offer them that degree of freedom and support.

Therapeutic houses create a counselling context which may be sufficient for very troubled clients who might otherwise stagnate on a diet of routine care but little attention. A good account of the depth of work which can be achieved within the context of a therapeutic house is given in Barnes and Berke (1991). That text illustrates a form of working which most practitioners would have to dismiss because they simply would not be prepared to make the degree of commitment which Joe Berke made to his client Mary Barnes.

My own experience of working in a therapeutic house is nearly twenty years old, but it does represent that kind of hard-earned lesson which is concomitant with apprenticeship. The patient was

John, a thirty-year-old, so-called psychotic for most of his post-adolescent life. My senior counsellor, Bob, worked with John for one hour each day from Monday to Saturday in the therapeutic house. One of John's most important possessions was a razor, which he had used on himself in a variety of ways. This was the latest in a long line of razors. After four months of working in a therapeutic house, John asked Bob to carry his razor for him. Bob was instructed that he must not lose the razor, and that he must bring it with him every day. Bob accepted the commitment on condition that he could send a replacement person on Sundays. As junior colleague with no family, that task fell to me. Each Sunday at 4.00 pm I would arrive at John's room. He would get out of bed, sit on the floor, and hold out his hands to receive the razor. I would sit on the floor opposite him and hand him the razor. Each time he breathed a hugh sigh of relief, and for the next hour he would hold the razor, sometimes fondling it like a baby. At the end of the hour, I held out my hands and he gave me the razor before returning to bed. This pattern continued for several months, during which Bob managed to depart for a three-week vacation, with me completing my normal Sunday assignation on each of those twenty-one days.

In all our time together, neither John nor I spoke one word to each other. He spoke with his counsellor Bob, but I was not his counsellor: I was simply part of the therapeutic context for John.

After a total of eight months in the therapeutic house, John began to emerge. He asked for the return of his razor and took it to a pawnbroker (John had even retrieved a sense of humour!).

John later wrote extensively about his experience of the work with Bob. In particular he stressed the importance of Bob's commitment and creativity, and also of the creation of an environment that supported rather than stressed him. As a part of that environment, he mentioned 'this small guy who came every Sunday to give me my razor'. John did not remember my name, probably because it was not me as a person or me as a counsellor that was important – my importance was only as a part of his therapeutic context.

The lesson for me from work with John, Bill, and traumatized war veterans is on the importance of the strength and consistency of my commitment to the client. Facing the possibility of change is serious business for the client, so the commitment I offer must also be serious. That commitment is a crucial element in the sufficiency of the therapeutic context.

On the dangers of under- and over-involvement

In the last section, reference was made to the danger of counselling becoming institutionalized, with rigid boundaries being drawn ever more narrowly. The same can happen on an individual level, with counsellors offering only limited contracts and working with clients in a progressively more detached way. Fortunately, the unique emphasis which our profession places upon supervision gives us a forum for highlighting such deterioration and facing the issues involved.

One of the ways in which such a personal crisis manifested itself for me occurred quite recently in relation to physical contact with clients. I come from a traditional Scots upbringing, which regards touching of any kind as inappropriate male behaviour, at least where it is linked with feelings of warmth, closeness, concern, or empathy. In my American training I struggled to overcome this handicap, and eventually had attained the level of a functioning amateur with respect to touching. For me, a gentle touch of the hand or shoulder of a client was about my limit; however, I was satisfied with that degree of physical contact because even those relatively small ways of touching can be enormously powerful in communicating warmth.

One of the recent factors which began to limit my ability to be in physical contact with clients was my growing awareness of counsellor, psychotherapist, and psychiatrist sexual abuse of clients and patients. This awareness had a big influence on me, and included some generalized feeling of guilt about my sex in relation to this work. I even found myself asking the question, 'Can men be counsellors, or does mainstream male socialization make us inappropriate for this profession?'

A second influence upon me was the vociferous criticism I received from other practitioners about references I made to physical contact in my writing and lecturing. This criticism ranged from those who regarded me as 'naïve' to others who used the word 'abusive' to describe my holding a client's hand. It must be said that almost all this criticism came from practitioners who operate within the psychodynamic framework, and no criticism came from clients themselves.

I found that this criticism and my own awareness of male abuse began to affect my practice considerably. I completely stopped having any kind of physical contact with clients, and I suspect that I closed down a little in general, particularly with respect to expressing warmth and intimacy, both of which are important ingredients for a person-centred practitioner.

The hard-earned lesson from this came from my clients, whose criticism helped me to break out of my self-imposed spell. From time to time I encourage clients to exchange views with me on what we are doing and how we are experiencing each other. It was at these times that clients took the opportunity to challenge me, sometimes on their experience of my detachment, and also on the lack of physical contact. Clients experienced this lack of contact sometimes as confusing, sometimes as rejecting, and occasionally even as abusive. Their comments included:

● 'It's as though you're only partially here . . . as though you're not at ease with yourself or that you're not at ease with me. I shift from believing one or the other of these depending on how bad I feel about myself!'
● 'It's as though there is an invisible wall between us that neither of us must breach.'
● 'When I was in despair one week, even the gentlest touch would have shown me that you were really there. I found myself drying up and feeling embarrassed for the whole of the next week . . . I think this is the first time that I've been really open since then.'
● 'I'm sensitive to touching – perhaps because I was abused as a child. I know the difference between okay and not-okay touching, and I need plenty of the okay stuff. The last thing an abused woman needs is to be treated like she is unclean and can't be touched.'
● 'I found your complete avoidance of touching to be almost abusive at times. It felt as though I was totally naked and you had all your clothes on – I mean, if felt like you were a voyeur.'

Listening to my clients, as well as getting a lot of support from my training colleagues has helped me to open out once again and to use myself more fully. The caution about inappropriate physical contact is always there, and it is right that it should be, for there is nothing worse than abusiveness in a counsellor. But that caution within the profession should not become so dominant that it suffocates, else we will have created such an impersonal, detached way of working that our clients will experience the abusiveness of our under-involvement.

In an earlier book in this series (Mearns and Dryden, 1990), Laura Allen wrote a chapter entitled 'A Client's Experience of Failure'. In that she described what for her was the abusiveness of under-involvement on the part of her counsellor:

At times I literally felt without skin, and experienced the physical pain that might go with that. I was feeling as vulnerable as that and he gave me absolutely nothing. I think just one smile and cuddle would have melted me – it would have brought such peace. Instead, the way he treated me was just a more subtle version of the abuse I had already had in my life. My father had been cruel to me in a physical way, by beating me, but this man did not even need to touch me to bully me.

I remind myself to be aware that under-involvement as well as over-involvement can be abusive in the experience of clients. The lesson for me is about exaggerating the importance of professional concerns to the extent that they unduly limit what I offer the client. I imagine that this is one of those learnings which I shall need to relearn many times over. Also, in writing this piece I have become acutely aware of how difficult it is to be a male in this profession. Sometimes I still despair about that.

On the balance between tyranny and the appropriate use of power in counselling

'I am going to pay you for three sessions. It may take less than that, but under no circumstances will I come back for a fourth session.' Andrew's voice was trembling with what looked like a mixture of anger and fear. Andrew, my new sixty-year-old client, had an unusual way of beginning our work together. He went on to describe his feelings about the previous twenty-seven years of weekly work with his former psychotherapist:

> I was afraid of him for twenty-seven years. After all that time I don't know a damn thing about him. I've no idea what he felt about our work, and I don't even know whether he liked me or not. I would hang on to his every word, taking any clue I could on whether he liked me or not – the next week could be joy or despair depending on the clues I got . . . He led me up so many blind alleys – we would spend weeks on things that seemed important to him. Sometimes I made things up that I knew would please him – I would invent dreams knowing the way he would interpret them.

Andrew's anger had erupted several months after his twenty-seven years' psychotherapy experience had ended. I asked Andrew if he would be able to revisit his psychotherapist, but he was most doubtful about that, expressing fears that he might become 'trapped' again if he went back. Andrew kept to his contract of three sessions and I have not seen him since. He used me as a context in which to vent his anger, while keeping me carefully at arm's length.

Andrew never knew the nerve he had touched in me. The picture he had painted of his psychotherapist represented an extreme of the tyranny which I fear above all else in the profession of counselling and psychotherapy.

Without doubt this abhorrence of misused power was what led me to a specialism in the person-centred approach to counselling. The choice was the right one in the sense that the person-centred approach has the mechanisms to monitor the power dynamics within the counselling relationship, but I made the same mistake that many others do when they come naïvely to person-centred working: I misunderstood the whole issue of power, feeling that I was working in a person-centred way if I minimized the amount of my own power which I used. In those early times I hid behind the person-centred label and functioned in a very unobtrusive way. I was certainly safe from the possibility of tyrannizing my client, but I was in danger of disappearing into the wallpaper! I conformed beautifully to that person-centred stereotype which is dominant in Britain: I was very warm and acceptant, had a rather wooden understanding of empathy, and not the slightest clue of what congruence really meant. When a client asked, 'What might happen to me if . . .?', I would give no answer except to turn it back to him. After numerous hard-earned lessons from clients, I gradually learned that I could give quite a lot in response, though not in answer, to that question: there are many things which may happen to him, and I know a fair number of them. I shall never forget a client who said to me, 'Why don't you just give me your wisdom and let *me* decide whether it's any use to me!'

Gradually, I learned that the power issue in person-centred counselling is not about me holding back on my expertise, but is concerned with creating a relationship which is empowering for my client. My power does not necessarily detract from my client's power unless I work in ways which have a disempowering effect upon him. As a working guideline, I would want to avoid what I call the four ingredients of tyranny: interpreting my client's behaviour within my own framework; interpreting my client's experiencing within my own framework; concealing my own experiencing; and failing to monitor my client's experience of our relationship.

Creating an empowering relationship involves avoiding the ingredients of tyranny and developing the facilitative conditions carefully researched in the theory of therapy within the person-centred approach. These are described in detail in one of the first books in the series (Mearns and Thorne, 1988). Avoiding tyranny does not mean that I have to withhold my own power – far from it, I must use my personal power to the full. It is the direction of that power which is the issue. If it is directed towards exercising and validating my belief system, increasing my power over my client, then it is in danger of becoming tyrannical. However, if it is directed towards my client becoming his own locus of evaluation, then it is likely to be empowering.

The lesson I have learned is that when the relationship is right in terms of empowerment, then both the client and myself can use our power to the full because neither need fear the other or ourselves. This ideal describes a state of mutuality within the relationship. When this is achieved, both parties experience enormous freedom as well as power. Interestingly, the achievement of this state of mutuality can bring a lightness and humour into the proceedings, as evidenced by this extract:

> *Client:* So what do you think I should do – should I tell my boss to keep his rotten job, or should I eat humble pie?
> *Counsellor:* That's an awful big question to have only two answers.
> *Client:* Smart-ass! You're avoiding the question again. What should I do?
> *Counsellor:* Eat humble pie.
> *Client:* You picked the wrong one.
> *Counsellor:* I know I picked the wrong one.
> *Client:* Clever bastard!

Conclusion

As well as the individual messages contained within these five hard-earned lessons, there seem to be two general themes reflected across them.

One theme is about balance: for instance, balance with respect to the usefulness of theory. Excessive theorizing can be obstructive, as in the first lesson, but inadequate understanding of theory can also be diminishing, as exemplified in the second lesson. Similarly, the importance of balance in relation to the degree and nature of my involvement is the subject of lesson four, while balance is also an issue in lesson five on power, though it is more the direction of the power which is the central message in that lesson.

The second theme, and the one which I find more challenging, is implied in lessons one, three, four, and five. These carry the suggestion that potentially I can learn more from my clients than from other counsellors. At first sight this conclusion seems so obvious as to be trite, yet I know how easy it is to forget. I know that it is much safer, more exciting, and self-aggrandizing to engage in case discussion with counselling colleagues than with my client. In case discussion with colleagues, I can elicit their reinforcing and similarly practitioner-centred perspective while at the same time displaying my clever analyses. This game may help myself and my colleagues to maintain and enhance our self-esteem, but I wonder how much more helpful it would be to engage in that same discussion with the client.

Perhaps I have written myself out of a job. In effect, the central message of this latter theme would suggest that the counsellor who is reading this book might learn more by closing it now and asking her client how he experiences her and their work together!

References

Barnes, M. and Berke, J. (1991) *Mary Barnes: Two Accounts of a Journey Through Madness*. London: Free Association Books.

Mearns, D. and Dryden, W. (eds) (1990) *Experiences of Counselling in Action*. London: Sage.

Mearns, D. and Thorne, B. (1988) *Person-Centred Counselling in Action*. London: Sage.

Rowan, J. (1990) *Subpersonalities*. London: Routledge.

7 Pat Milner

I was born and educated in Lancashire, and this is still clearly evident in my speech. I was a teacher, and moved into counselling from a background of education twenty-six years ago, which means that some of these hard-earned lessons are drawn from my experience of counselling in schools and universities.

My first counselling training was a diploma course at Reading University, and two years later I went as a Fulbright Scholar to the United States for further training and experience. On my return to England in 1969, I started the Student Counselling Service at University College London.

In 1970 I became the founder Chairman(!) of the Association for Student Counselling, and published my first book *Counselling in Education* (1974). In the same year I began my association with the South West London College Counselling Courses, run by Brigid Proctor, and in 1977 became a full-time tutor there. This was a continuation of pioneering work in the counselling field, for the SWLC courses were trail-blazers in the presentation of counselling training in experiential, self-directed learning communities where staff and students together planned the courses and assessed the students' work.

A viral illness leading to ME forced my retirement from SWLC on health grounds in 1983, and for three years I was not able to work, but I have recently returned to counselling in a part-time, freelance role, combining counselling, supervision, and an element of training at Goldsmiths' College and the Centre for Stress Management in Blackheath.

My counselling orientation is based on a foundation of the person-centred approach, but illness has produced some iconoclastic tendencies which mix and match Egan's skills, psychodynamic insights, and, very occasionally, the practical, cognitive-behavioural skills of working with post-traumatic stress disorder and the management of stress.

Self-preservation and the counsellor

This hard-earned lesson emphasizes for me the difficulty some of us who become counsellors have in taking sufficient care of ourselves: the almost automatic way in which we put our own needs last, and the long-term cost of our lack of self-preservation.

My nature and my nurturing in combination produced the stoical workaholic that is me – not all of me, but that flagellating fusion of characteristics which led me to pitch myself non-stop into work. Because I was blessed with a strong body and am a stubborn Taurean, I was enabled to live and work in overdrive for many years, without taking much care of myself, and, apparently, without paying too high a price.

There are several experiences which I could have used to learn to be different. As a school counsellor, I tended to want to do everything and cope with every challenge which came my way. During one winter, we had such deep snow that public transport stopped and I could not get my car on to the road because it was completely buried in a snow drift. I lived out in the country, about six miles from the school, and without thinking I walked to work through all the snow because I had appointments with clients, leaving home at about six-thirty in the morning, and reaching the school at about half-past ten, quite exhilarated. The wise head asked if he could speak to me privately, and said gently, 'You should not have come in today. Don't push yourself so hard.' I heard his words, and his genuine concern touched me deeply; I did have time to think about them because just two of my clients were in school. His message had strong opposition from deeper, earlier voices, which were full of 'musts' and 'shoulds' and 'oughts'.

Subsequently, when I worked with students at an American university for a year, I worked and studied for a master's degree, getting high grades – of course! – and continued to pay the mortgage on my house in England. I completed the year with a master's degree in counselling – and a duodenal ulcer.

At the end of a long Saturday spent commuting to and from Hampshire, chairing the proceedings of the AGM of the Association for Student Counselling, lunching with members and having a meal with some of them at the end of the day, I was genuinely surprised when a visiting Australian counsellor said he expected I would have Monday off because he thought the day had been a 'punishing programme'.

I see the same look of genuine surprise cross the faces of some counsellors and some students of counselling when I suggest that some of their days are equally punishing. The hard-earned lesson, with the clarity of hindsight, is that people like me, who tend to want to do everything and cope with everything and are inwardly driven to do this over many years, are likely to be brought to a standstill by some kind of powerful intervention, such as illness. Through many pioneering years of exciting, yet draining, challenge, I failed to balance my resources, and consistently expended more than I was generating, without recognizing that this was inappropriate and not in my interests. My conservation skills were negligible, and I could not admit that my prodigal enthusiasm, mixed with my stoical endurance, would not last for ever.

It took a viral illness, which resulted in ME and three years in the wilderness, to reveal the very obvious truth that my resources are finite, and my profligate live-now-pay-later approach to work left me with a debt that I will probably be repaying for the rest of my life.

My concern now is for conservation both in the wider world context of rain forests and elephants, and also in the micro-world of people and their personal resources. I am forced to conserve to be able to work, and have developed a style of concise, rather abrupt, sometimes epigrammatic comments to students which have become known, I hope with some affection, as 'Pat's one-liners'. These derive from my challenging attempts to encourage counsellors to conserve their resources, by not over-burdening themselves with tasks and commitments, and by contracting to take care of themselves through exercise, relaxation, treats, holidays or breaks, or whatever they enjoy that replenishes their energy sources. Some recent examples of these one-liners are:

- Respect the client as thyself – if you are not able to respect yourself by taking care of your 'self', what effect does this have on your clients?
- Counselling is interesting, demanding and seductive – beware the dangers of promiscuity.
- Your tape was good enough, it got you into the second year, forget it – your life is too pressurized for you to usefully 'back job' in this way.
- Supervision is a reward – it supports us in learning about ourselves, our clients and our work in the company of someone who cares about us.

One way in which I teach by example is to announce, several times a year, that I am about to fly off to a Mediterranean island whose people are artistic and musical. They shout down the streets at each other by way of communication – no careful distillation of words here – the sun normally shines, people don't listen much and I find its powers of reconstitution inestimable.

Holidays are good periodic restorers; day-by-day care and monitoring of resources seems more difficult for me to manage, yet it is vital. I really need to make an appointment with myself each week to talk to 'me' about taking care of myself. You do this for your clients – can you equally respect yourself?

Culture, concepts, and language

It is a salutary experience to realize that the concepts and language which we readily share as counsellors do not find a ready acceptance nor a mutual understanding among our clients. If those clients also have different cultural origins from our own, this dissonance may be heightened and prove a real barrier to effective work. I think we have a clear responsibility as counsellors to improve our cross-cultural knowledge and competence.

Three vignettes illustrate this hard-earned lesson – I was obviously a slow learner here! Indeed, in all three cases it was my slowness in grasping the crucial cultural import which blocked the effectiveness of the communication and therefore of the counselling work.

The first client was a young man from an Asian family who was living in a mixed hall of residence at university. He said that his studies were going quite well, he did feel a bit homesick, but the aspect of his life which he most wanted to talk about was his newly discovered attractiveness to women. When we looked at this in more detail, he described, excitedly, how in the dining-room the women students found him irresistibly attractive and really encouraged him to flirt with them. However, when he responded, he felt they quickly rejected him.

It actually took me several sessions to grasp the significance, for him, of being looked in the eye by women. His cultural and personal experience had been that women looked at men with lowered eyes, which meant that when the women students looked at him openly, and talked in a friendly way at the meal table, he became sexually aroused. When he tried to make the interaction more private and intimate by asking one of the women to coffee in his room or to see a film with him, they declined his invitation and he felt spurned and angry.

It was not until he became angry with me and said, 'And you do it too', that I recognized that by maintaining good eye contact in our counselling sessions, I was compounding his difficulty. Although I modified my eye contact and did not hold his gaze so often or for such a length of time, we ended our work in exasperation because he could not accept that I did not want a sexual relationship with him. My eyes had betrayed me!

The second client was a post-graduate student from Ethiopia who was referred by his GP because he was becoming increasingly distressed and agitated by reading about the outbreak of civil war in his country and seeing it reported on television here. He was adamant that his countrymen would not fight each other, was convinced that all the English newspapers were telling lies, and believed that the television reporters were enemies of his people.

He could not accept the opportunity to ring his family from the counselling service, nor could he talk to other students from his own country. It was as if his memories of home had to be preserved intact, lest he himself should disintegrate. Although I could empathize with his distress, I did not share his perception of the situation. My mistake was not to make this clear to him. By reflecting what he felt and what he said, while inwardly believing that his perceptions were not reality, I added to his confusion. For him, my reflections were agreement, because his cultural experience was that if you did not agree you argued about it and said that you did not agree.

When I said, 'It seems difficult for you to believe that your countrymen would fight each other', he heard me say, 'I don't believe your countrymen would fight each other.' It is important not to assume that clients necessarily hear what we say, particularly clients from different cultures, or differing areas of our own culture, or those for whom English is not their first language.

The third story concerns a lady from the Philippines who had been living in London for about four years and was married to an older, divorced English man. They had two young children of their own, and also had the husband's two children on alternate weekends. He would visit his former wife and children on the intervening weekend. My client thought she was being used, and put into the role of 'servant', but said she did not know how to change things.

We worked together for a couple of sessions in her home, exploring the cultural shock she experienced in England, working on how she might negotiate with her husband on the areas in which she wanted change. At one stage I shared the idea that the two of us might learn together about the cultural differences, since she knew about the Philippines and I knew about England. This was obviously too much of a culture shock for her. She rang the centre from which I was working as a volunteer and said she did not want to work with a learner, could she please have an expert!

The hard-earned lessons from these three examples show that, in the first, our quite valid reliance on the messages of non-verbal communication, and in particular eye contact, needs to be checked out. We cannot assume that clients from our own culture will share our understanding of non-verbal communication, and we certainly cannot assume such shared meanings from people with different cultural experiences.

The second lesson underlines the fact that people are generally not aware that our use of the skills of reflection, paraphrasing, and summarizing are ways of checking that we have understood what they are saying. They may assume that these are ways in which we show that we agree with what they are saying, as did my Ethiopian client.

The third client was not at all familiar with the idea that counselling can be a shared learning experience, and because I did not explain this, or because she did not want such an experience, she took charge very firmly and ended our work together.

Mediation and confidentiality

While the concept of confidentiality is a central tenet of counselling theory, the maintenance of confidentiality in practice is not necessarily a straightforward issue, especially for new counsellors. This particular hard-earned lesson comes from my early counselling experience in a comprehensive school. I experienced some difficulty in a establishing a *modus vivendi* between what I had been taught about confidentiality and the working alliance, which is particularly crucial in education, where young people are dependent upon the guidance and understanding of adult staff for their progress through the school system.

My client was Mary, a bright, shy, fifteen year old, regarded by several heads of department who taught her as having the potential and the wish to go on to university. It was one of the heads of department who referred Mary to me because, although she was still working well in school, she seemed unhappy and 'not her usual self', as he put it.

Mary told me she was struggling at home, trying to care for her mother, who for several weeks had been not only afraid to leave the house herself, but also did not want to be left alone in it during the day. Her mother became very agitated and distressed each morning when her husband left for work and Mary and her brother went to school.

The burden of care was largely borne by Mary, who had become regularly half an hour late for registration, and was therefore detained after school in line with her house head's disciplinary policy. The detention added to her problems because it meant that she was late home, which again raised her mother's anxiety. Mary asked if I would speak to her house head, who did not accept her explanation of her lateness, which was that her mother was unwell. Thus Mary was asking me to mediate on her behalf, but she did not want the details of her mother's situation shared with anyone else because her mother had sworn her to secrecy, which she had already broken by telling me.

Although I was not confident about this counsellor/mediator role, I did speak to the house head about Mary's situation, choosing my words carefully, in case I said too much. His response was not co-operative, and he said he would need to have a note from her mother or father to put on his files, since it was all a cock-and-bull story anyway, and I was just gullible.

This put Mary and me back to square one, since her mother wanted to keep her at home and so would not write such a letter, and her father could not write. Mary and I talked about getting medical help for her mother, who was adamant she would not have the doctor call, nor visit him herself. We decided on a risky two-part plan: I would introduce myself to the family GP by telephone to alert him, and I would also write a note for the house head. The GP was understandably most suspicious of my call, but was eventually the pivotal person in the dilemma because he knew that Mary's mother had suffered similar difficulties about two years before, and said he would visit her.

My letter to the house head was clearly headed 'Confidential', and was addressed to him personally. In it I said simply that there were problems of illness at home, confirmed by the family GP, which would make it difficult for Mary to arrive in time for registration for the next two weeks, until the end of term. Would he excuse her lateness and waive the detention for that period?

The following day he called down a busy corridor to me at break-time, 'I've got your letter about Mary. If I let her get away with being late, everybody will think they can do it.' By this time I had closed the gap between us and was standing next to him, and we eventually agreed quietly that he would not impose detention and would tell her tutor of his decision.

A couple of days later, Mary's tutor put her head round my door and said, 'I know about Mary's difficulties and won't report her lateness, but do you know that your confidential letter is pinned on the noticeboard outside the house head's office!' I was able to act upon my anger by removing the letter from the noticeboard, by challenging the house head, and eventually having regular meetings with all the house heads to talk about procedures concerning issues like confidentiality and referrals.

Mary saw the experience as a distressing betrayal of her trust, which my apology could not alter. Her mother accepted a domiciliary visit from a psychiatrist and did get well again, which had been what Mary hoped for, but I was left with questions about my role and actions in the situation. Was it appropriate to have intervened so actively in the life of Mary and her family, by communicating with the GP, and also by writing a letter *in loco parentis* to account for Mary's lateness? Would it have been more helpful to work with Mary alone, in more of a 'pure' counselling role, without any mediation or intervention in her difficulties with her house head, or her mother's illness? My immediate reaction was to conclude that I had been too active, and I retreated into a safer 'purer' style of counselling, going on to work with students and adults with whom such a style is indicated.

With the benefit of hindsight, I now look back twenty-five years and think that Mary and I together decided on a joint course of action. True, we did not foresee all the consequences in that we were both shocked by the breaking of confidentiality by the house head. Mary's concerns had been to make things right for herself in school, to get her mother well, and to protect her reputation among people who had a cruel attitude to mental illness, and we achieved some of these outcomes. However, uncertainty about confidentiality and protection of reputation has much more serious consequences in those major areas of children's lives which concern physical, emotional, and sexual abuse.

The hard-earned lesson is that agreed mediation on behalf of clients, particularly those who are not independent adults, is sometimes an appropriate activity for a counsellor, but it inevitably blurs the boundaries of confidentiality because we cannot assume that other professional people will necessarily respect that confidentiality. Some, of course, will do so, and others will not, and education is one of the areas which does not yet have a clear statement of ethical practice.

Elizabeth Jones, HMI, stressed this point at a recent BAC conference on 'Interpersonal and Counselling Skills – Needs for 1990s', which was reported in the BAC journal *Counselling*:

> There is as yet no Code of Ethical Practice in Education which would protect any confidentiality of disclosed personal information. It is likely that the existence of such a code would help to build up trust in an educational setting, enabling pupils to impart the personal information which is needed to give them the help they seek.

Experience has taught me to be realistic about people's inexperience in handling confidentiality. I would work for the same outcomes for Mary, but I would not now be so craven in the face of the house head's needs for written information. Instead, I would use assertion skills to work with him verbally on his needs for the power of the written information, and to sort out the issues between his role as house head and mine as counsellor, and those between him as a person, and me as a person.

The intrinsic nature of the counselling setting

In the 1970s, the writings and talks of R. D. Laing represented an innovative, apparently more humane, alternative approach to the area of mental health and mental illness, which did not rely on the traditional medical model.

I had recently been impressed by a presentation from staff of one of the therapeutic communities based on Laing's approach when I saw for counselling a student from a neighbouring college, who was referred to me by her tutor. The referral was made by telephone, and I was reluctant to take it because I was already very busy working with students from my own college. Allowing myself to be persuaded to see the student was my first mistake.

When Penny arrived for her appointment, I was surprised to see that she was accompanied by her tutor, and it was clear there was a powerful, interdependent relationship between the two of them, in which the tutor – a middle-aged man – was clearly out of his depth. Penny had a substantial presence. She was big and heavy in build, and I felt she was burdened both physically and emotionally. She dwarfed her tutor, who was small, slightly built, and very agitated. Because Penny and her tutor came together, I spoke to them both briefly, and then saw her separately before bringing in her tutor for the last ten minutes, at her request.

When I enquired why Penny's tutor had accompanied her, they both said she suffered from agoraphobia and could not go out on her own. My suggestion was that she would probably find referral to a cognitive behaviour therapist helpful, but this was turned down by Penny, who said there were family issues she wanted to work on, and she would like to work with me. I pointed out that this would involve making the journey once a week on her own, and asked if she was prepared to do that. She said she would come if her tutor came with her, which he eagerly agreed to do. I firmly said this was not acceptable, since it was important she take responsibility for getting herself to counselling, if it was to work, and I was sorry but I could not help her.

I thought that it was clearly important to establish some firm boundaries with Penny and her tutor, because the confusion in their relationship was rendering him helpless and her omnipotent, to the detriment of both. I gave Penny two referral sources, one medical and one cognitive behavioural, with a strong recommendation that she pursue one of them.

About three weeks later, I saw Penny's name in my diary for an appointment. She had telephoned to make the appointment herself, and told me when she arrived that she had come alone, in a taxi.

Since she had come on my terms, I felt obliged to fulfil my part of the contract and see her, although I felt very uneasy about doing so. Remembering the boundary issue, I initiated a contract to work for six sessions, which would bring her up to the start of her exams, and then to review.

Our sessions varied from talking about her family situation and her concerns and feelings about that, to entering together a most bizarre and delicate world made entirely of glass, which was first presented as the realm of her dreams, and then as her waking reality. These were times of incredible intensity and fearfulness for both of us.

My supervisor was keen that I should refer Penny to a psychiatrist, and when she declined to be referred, strongly urged that I should stop working with her because she was clearly too ill for counselling to be of help; in his view she would probably have to be admitted to hospital. My rational mind fully agreed; however, in my own way I had become as fascinated by Penny and her world as her tutor had been. I was torn between the 'ideal' of a therapeutic community approach and my supervisor's alternative of hospitalization.

With hindsight, I was not providing a therapeutic community in one session a week, and yet the work Penny and I did had that quality. She began to get very agitated about the paintings in my room, saying she thought the figures in them would harm me, and I remember I stayed very clear and calm and appreciated her concern, but said I had chosen those paintings with great care and that the figures in them felt very loving to me and not threatening.

Although in our work together I was empathic and calm, Penny began to occupy my thoughts and emotional energy to such an extent outside the sessions that I began to feel quite ill. I could not sleep for thinking about her, and my work became ragged and unfocused because Penny's presence was constantly in my head. Because of this I made an extra appointment with my supervisor.

When Penny did not come for her last appointment, I had become so personally involved that I was overwhelmed by very powerful feelings. I was angry with her, I was concerned for her well-being, I was fearful for myself and my sanity, and felt very fragile. My supervisor was supportive and encouraged me to find out if I could what had happened to Penny because he was concerned for both of us. In my anxiety I rang the hostel where Penny stayed three times without being able to speak to her because she was out. I wrote to her, saying I was sorry she had not been able to keep her appointment and that I would keep the same time available for her the following week. I also telephoned her tutor, who was not in college, so I left a brief message asking him to ring me.

All this activity was out of character. I did not usually pursue students who did not keep appointments, and I certainly did not contact their tutors – but this was different. There was no response from Penny herself, but two weeks later her tutor left a message to say that Penny had taken her exams and gone home, and he was flying to America for the summer. I felt relieved because I knew Penny had a supportive doctor at home, and I did feel able to let her go at this point. However, my withdrawal symptoms were such that I had to take time out and go away to recollect myself. Gradually, the panic attacks became fewer, and by the autumn, after some counselling myself, I felt quite grounded again, and saw things differently.

What I saw differently was that I needed to restrict my responsibility for offering counselling to members of my own college. This meant that I stopped taking referrals from students or staff of other colleges who did not have counsellors – they had to be responsible for their own students. I saw too that a counselling service could not be a therapeutic community, but that it could provide a therapeutic oasis in an academic community, and that was what some students sought and needed in order to proceed through college life.

Another hard-earned realization was that it was not possible for me to provide such a therapeutic oasis for students who were as troubled as Penny had been by powerfully disturbing thoughts and feelings without being overwhelmed myself. I have some difficulty in accepting the combination of drug treatment and counselling for clients who endure the condition called schizophrenia because of their antipathetic outcomes. It is not surprising that one of the drugs in use is called the 'liquid cosh' as it certainly knocks out the disturbing thoughts, feelings and most of the others as well, which mitigates against working in a counselling way. However, my post-Penny compromise was to accept that for some people, the combination of carefully monitored drug treatment, which enabled students to stay in college rather than hospital, and counselling offered a better chance of growth towards a positive future than either approach on its own.

Twenty years on from Laing's creative work we do not have a host of therapeutic communities in which people can be supported as they take out from everyday life to work through their confusion, agitation, and extraordinary inner worlds. Indeed, the capacity of even the traditional psychiatric communities is being reduced. Nevertheless, a therapeutic community as described by

Laing and an academic community have very different functions, and the people who work in them have different responsibilities and skills. If I am to be helpful I need to stay in touch with my own limits and boundaries and to think and speak clearly with an objective compassion. I cannot safely venture into the seductive and confused world of people whose reality appears bizarre because my own bizarreness is too readily released and I become fearful and lose my way.

What Penny forced me to learn is that while I may have admired the ideals of Laing, I could not carry them out in an academic setting, and needed to find a compromise which allowed my survival. The setting in which counselling takes place is as intrinsic a component of the work as the people involved.

The client who does not want to work

It is a sound general principle of counselling that clients will choose the issues and concerns upon which they want to work in their sessions. Notwithstanding the counsellor's responsibility to challenge such things as omissions, discrepancies, and distortions, this general principle usually works well.

However, there are occasionally people who come into counselling in the hope of avoiding the reality of their lives, and who seek to enlist the counsellor's help in removing some of the obstacles in their path. I have not always been perceptive in noticing this reluctance to work, and have in the past been too ready to make excuses for people who presented themselves as victims. Sometimes such clients can be recognized because they recall various other people they have been to see, and their dilemma may be summarized as, 'I've seen all these people and none of them could help.' It is tempting, though not realistic, for me to think that I may be effective where others apparently have not, and I have fallen into this trap on more than one occasion.

I think these falls into flattery have helped me to develop a warning system which leads me to consider carefully whether or not I will choose to work with a client who presents in this challenging way. However, the experience I had with Betty was one of those occasions upon which I needed to proceed carefully and failed to do so.

Betty came to see me privately because she had a friend who had seen me and found it '*so* helpful'. She had been to the university counselling service because she had not been well enough to take her third-year exams. When asked to be specific, she described symptoms similar to those of glandular fever. Betty said the university counsellor had not been able to help, and that she would have to re-sit her exams in September in order to continue to the final year of the course. In response to my enquiries, Betty said that she felt too ill to study for her exams, and, yes, she had had a blood test but the results had been lost.

When Betty went home at the end of term, she had seen her GP, who had sent her for another blood test. But he really did not seem to appreciate how ill she felt. She could not talk to her parents, they just did not understand her, and she told me she had always felt picked on at school by certain teachers. The only person who knew the 'real Betty' was a boyfriend she had lived with in France when studying there in her second year. She missed him very much, and described their relationship as tempestuous and argumentative.

At the end of our first session, we made a contract to work for three sessions, at a reduced fee because Betty was a student. We were to look at her immediate future choices concerning continuing her course or possibly returning to France to be with her boyfriend. Then, in the last five minutes, she introduced the idea of getting a job in the music business, which was, of course, 'What I really want to do.'

Betty arrived ten minutes before the second session was due to end, saying she had 'missed the train'. I said clearly that our appointment had been for four o'clock, and that it was not now possible for us to work that day. I re-stated the date and time of our next appointment, checked that she had written it down, and said I would see her then.

Betty arrived promptly, to the minute, for her next session. She was evasive and placatory about her lateness of the week before, and I floundered between my irritation and an empathy with her struggle with her own elusiveness. We talked more about her choices and her thoughts and feelings around them, but always ended in the same place, with Betty listing her parents, teachers, the university counsellor and the GP, all of whom just made life so difficult for her by their inability to understand.

When I reflected upon the one-sided responsibility in all these relationships and tried to encourage Betty to look at her own interaction in them, she suddenly started to tell me she really wondered if she was schizophrenic. She said she had actually heard voices in her head in bed, and she had read about schizophrenia in the books in the university library. My summary at the end of the session made the point that we cannot change the other people in Betty's life who she feels are so unhelpful. However, we can begin to help her make some decisions and take responsibility for them herself, so that she does not feel so badly let down by others. She agreed enthusiastically.

Betty did not return for her third session, but sent a card of apology with many thanks for all my help! Looking back, it is possible to see several clues in my interaction with Betty which indicated that our work together was likely to be difficult, if not actually set up to fail.

The first of these came early in the initial session when she told me that her friend had found working with me 'so helpful'. This was a fall into flattery on my part, the reality is that I am sometimes helpful as a counsellor, but never, '*so* helpful'. Had I picked up Betty's exaggeration for the sake of emphasis in her introduction, I would probably have been alerted to other aspects of her story, such as her feeling that her GP did not appreciate how ill she was. He had sent her for a second blood test, which was responsible, but he had 'failed her'. What had he failed to do?

A further clue as to how counselling might proceed came in Betty's feeling picked on and misunderstood by her parents, and sometimes her teachers. Had I picked this up at the time I might have pondered the fact that I too am an adult, like parents and teachers, and wondered whether or not my challenges would be regarded as 'picking on her'.

The only person who Betty felt really understood her was her French boyfriend, who was hundreds of miles away and not in regular contact. The importance of this lay in the reality for her that no one currently in her life seemed to understand her, and the reality for me, with hindsight, that I was not likely to appear any more understanding of her than did the other adults in her life, given our brief acquaintance. Betty's sudden introduction of both her interest in the music business and her concern about a possible schizophrenic condition were both ways of asking for help. Her arrival fifty minutes late for the second session gave an indication of her ambivalence in accepting the realities of such help.

I think Betty wanted to feel she was special, and tried hard through her behaviour to get special treatment from a variety of people, but her need ran up against the realities of life. Betty could only get into her final year at university by re-sitting her exams, that was the 'special treatment' she had been allowed, to take into account her possible glandular fever. She wanted to spend the summer in France with her boyfriend and return in time to start her final year. Working for her exams and re-sitting them in September might mean she would not do that.

Counselling was seen as a magic wand that would remove that reality, and I became another addition to the list of people who, in Betty's eyes, had not been able to help her and had not under-stood. I needed to convey two important things to Betty in our first session, both confronting the reality of our situation. The first was to summarize clearly the dilemma she presented by saying, 'You seem to want to complete your course which will involve re-sitting your exams and doing some work for that in the summer. You also would like to spend the summer in France with your boyfriend. Can you see how you might do both of these things?' The second was to say that I could not help her to avoid re-sitting her exams.

When clients present with a succession of people who have not been able to help, it is important to find out what it is they have not been able to help with. Counsellors are usually good at encouraging people to pursue positive goals and to increase their sense of what is possible in their lives. However, we are not God and we do not do miracles, and for some clients, the choice they prefer is not available – and sometimes we need to say that.

Conclusion

The issue which threads its way through all the experiences and examples in my hard-earned lessons is that of boundaries. In various forms, it is repeated like a musical theme. My introduction provides a few notes of this theme in its outline of my roots in Lancashire and the expansion of geographical and family boun-daries; in my trek south and my choice of counselling work, perceived by my family as new-fangled and without security. As for going to America, my grandfather had done that and returned penniless! Not a good idea.

'Self-preservation and the counsellor' presents the theme in a major way as it illustrates how my work has been dominant and out of balance with other aspects of my life, albeit in a challenging and rewarding way. We work hard to understand our clients, and there is a reminder of the importance of acknowledging, encounter-ing, and finding a way through the barriers of language and culture, together with a look at the inhibiting effects of our failure to notice the limits of our clients' understanding of us. I had shared in the fraught inner world of students before I worked with Penny, but the combination of end-of-year fatigue and the abrupt and early ending of our sessions left me stranded in my own inner world, and made it difficult for me to move back into working reality, until I had worked on myself. On reflection I see that Betty's testing and stretching of the boundaries of reality to fit her wants is a theme paralleled in my own life, which contributed to the frustration of our work together.

It seems as if the theme of my hard-earned lessons is that there is a parallel between the issues and concerns of my personal and working life and those of the limits which have surrounded some of the most difficult aspects of my learning about counselling.

8 John Rowan

The theoretical orientation to which I mainly hold is primal integration. It follows the work of Bill Swartley, Frank Lake, and Stan Grof, and lays the major stress upon early trauma as the basic cause of neurosis. Unlike the somewhat parallel approach of Arthur Janov, it puts great emphasis on the whole person – body, feelings, intellect, and spirit. It is a humanistic therapy in the fullest sense, based on the fundamental belief that the inner core of the client is ultimately healthy, and that it is only the defences that are unhealthy. This is the basic humanistic belief in the real self. This form of therapy makes use of active techniques from a number of sources – body, feeling, analysis and intuition – integrated into a strong theoretical framework. In line with this, I am particularly interested in the use of subpersonalities, a concept which is widespread under different names in most forms of psychotherapy. There is a full discussion of the whole theory in my book on the subject (1990).

Siding with the client

I wish to discuss one session in which I found myself contradicting one of my most basic assumptions. A section in one of my books has the heading 'The therapist is not a rescuer', and this seemed to me the ultimate wisdom in therapy: 'Every time I take responsibility for the client, I stop the client taking responsibility. Every time I try to help, I get in the client's way.' I was quite dogmatic about this, because it seemed to be so basic. I still think it is very important.

The session was with a client I shall call Sarah, a woman in her early thirties, recently married, about average height, dark, somewhat overweight. Her main problem seemed to be a sometimes very severe depression, though eating problems were also important at times. The depression had been serious enough to make her attempt suicide by cutting her wrists more than once, but she had never been hospitalized. She had been to a number of therapists before, and was taking a course to become a therapist herself.

Sarah's history was probably the worst I had ever come across. It started before her conception, which took place when her mother was forty years old. Her mother had just run away with Sarah's father after an unhappy marriage of fifteen years. Her husband was strongly opposed to children, and had made her have an abortion in the early days of the marriage. She had then talked him into having children, but after years of failure had been told she was infertile.

Sarah's father was a man of wide interests and varied talents, and twenty-five years older than her mother. He looked after her mother, who was in poor health with nervous complaints and poor nutrition. During the pregnancy, Sarah's mother was going through the stress of trying to get a divorce, to which her husband would not agree, and was consuming much black coffee and chain-smoking cigarettes all day.

Having been told she was infertile, Sarah's mother did not know she was pregnant. As she began to feel a lump in her womb, she assumed it must be a growth of some kind. She was very afraid of doctors, and would not go near them if possible. When the lump grew, she thought it must be cancer, but still did not want to go to a doctor. When it moved, she thought it must be a mobile cancerous growth of a particularly virulent kind. It appears that panic must have got through somehow to the foetus (Verny, 1982; Ridgway, 1987). In reconstruction, it seems that the chemical shock of these reactions coming into the foetus every time it moved actually conditioned it to move as little as possible, so that instead of a normally vigorous motion of the foetus in the womb, there were just a few rather restricted movements – ironically, just the sort of movements to confirm the mother in her beliefs.

Ten days before her birth, Sarah's mother had 'stomach pains' so bad that a doctor had to be called. He told her she was pregnant. This sent her into a new panic, because she felt she was too old to have a baby, and knew she had not been eating properly for the past few months.

The birth was prolonged and difficult, and the baby experienced anoxia and extreme paralysing terror as the walls of the uterus closed in and there seemed to be no way out. The mother's hair and nails dropped out after the birth, and she had no milk. The baby had two fingernails not properly developed, and the mother thought the child might be mentally deformed or retarded.

Sarah's mother had been brought up very strictly and religiously, and felt extremely guilty at having brought an illegitimate child into the world. As the baby grew, she saw it as fat, ugly, and badly behaved. She didn't like it. And so it went on, right up to the moment the mother died of cancer when Sarah was twenty-two years old. Sarah's father had died when she was nine.

The therapy

In the early days of the therapy, we spent most of the time on Sarah's mother, just following her feelings back into her childhood again and again. We found that her mother kept on turning up in the most extraordinary disguises, in dreams and in fantasies: for example, we spent some time wrestling with a 'death skeleton', which was extremely frightening and threatening, and this turned out in the end to be her mother again. One of the most fearful versions for Sarah was the Black Witch, which came up in dreams and fantasies, and actually laid a spell on the child Sarah to strike her dumb. This was a very accurate statement of what happened when Sarah's mother came on the scene: Sarah was dumbstruck.

For a long time it seemed that we were stuck, because Sarah could find no way of facing her mother without being overcome immediately. There seemed to be no strength, no resource within her that was strong enough to resist. She lost her voice; she couldn't think of anything to say or do; it was as if she were paralysed.

The event that triggered a change was a lecture which I went to on the work of John Rosen. The lecturer said that one of the problems Rosen had tackled successfully was a client who had an extremely heavy and punitive superego. It was as if the superego sat on top of the ego and squashed it, with such weight and force that the ego had no chance at all to respond or resist or retaliate in any way. What Rosen did was to line up with the client and throw his weight against the superego as well. This released more energy in the client, by giving explicit permission to answer back, as it were, and also by giving a model of how to do it.

Although in my theory there is no superego, and no ego either in the strict Freudian sense, I could see that the superego functioned just like a subpersonality. So I could understand what was being said in my own terms, and see the relevance of that to Sarah's case. Sarah also had a heavy and punitive subpersonality sitting on top of her and 'squashing' her.

But could I use this method? On the one hand it did fit in with my ideas about being imaginative and trying new things, but on the other hand it went right against my ideas about the client being autonomous and self-responsible. So it was as if one voice was saying 'Try it!', while another voice was saying, 'Don't you dare!'. In the event, my curiosity won out over my conscience. At the next opportunity, I lined up with Sarah against her mother. In my way of working, with Sarah sitting on one cushion and her mother (in what ever guise) on the other, this was in fact very easy to set up.

I simply put another cushion next to Sarah's and sat on it myself, saying things to support Sarah's own statements.

This did not work. Sarah's mother, or what I would call the bad mother subpersonality, was still too strong for both of us together. Again we had to retire, baffled, and frustrated. But something seemed to have shifted slightly, though I wasn't quite sure what it was. There was a definite movement, such that I felt that here was a promising approach, if only some way could be found of taking it further.

The session
The next time the opportunity arose, we were both more ready to grab it and use it constructively. We were working on a dream about a giant spider. Sarah had done a painting of the dream, which I have in front of me as I write. It shows a foetus in the middle of the page, pinkish on a blue background, with a huge purple umbilical cord going out to the left, through the red border of the womb, to a yellow moon hung in a night sky with yellow and silver stars. Below the sky, on the left of the picture, is a blue-green sea with smooth waves. On the right of the picture, filling the whole space, is a huge, black, hairy spider with red eyes and what look like two horns with knobs on the ends. The legs are too big to be contained on the page, and disappear over the edge of the paper to the right, and behind the womb to the left. The background on the right-hand side is red, except at the top, where it becomes red and yellow flames against a violet background. It looks like a sort of devil-spider. One of the legs curves right over the top of the spider's head, and looks almost like an alternative umbilical cord.

As I often do, after going through the dream and finding that the spider represented her mother, I suggested we put the spider on a cushion and talk to it. Sarah agreed to this, and we set it up, but I could see she was experiencing some fear. I remembered the previous incident where I had taken her side, and it suddenly occurred to me how we might make it work better this time.

This time I said, 'Now, there is a magic glass screen just here (I indicated a line) between you and the spider. You can talk to the spider, but the spider can't get through the screen. The spider can still hear and see and talk through the screen, but is completely blocked by the screen. You can get at the spider if you want to, but the spider can't get at you. And the screen will stay there until I take it down again.'

I lined up with Sarah as before, and supported her against the spider, shouting back at the spider that she had no right to attack Sarah, that Sarah had seen through her game, that she wasn't going to stand for it any more, and so on. This time, as we went back and forth between Sarah and the giant spider, the spider diminished in size and paled in colour. It became smaller and smaller and weaker and weaker, until Sarah felt capable of facing it and dealing with it herself.

For the first time, we had the feeling of victory against her mother. For the first time, her mother respected Sarah. We had broken through, and the positive feeling was tremendous. In talking with Sarah afterwards, she said that the magic screen was like a protection that made her feel safe. It made her feel that she was allowed to communicate. Before this, she had felt no right to communicate, particularly where her mother was concerned (the dumb-child motif mentioned earlier).

Of course, there were other things going on too. It may be felt that I was perhaps functioning on one level as a bigger magician than the Black Witch, and beating her on a magical level. At an unconscious level, perhaps I was her father come back to rescue her this time. Perhaps the glass screen was simply a schizoid defence, a temporary neurosis. Sarah's own view, expressed later, was that I was showing her how to talk back to her mother: she had no model or script for it, so did not know how to do it until she saw me do it. Once she had picked up the model, she was able to use it, and this seemed to break the dumbness spell put on the child by the Black Witch.

But as a therapist with the theory outlined above, I was in turmoil. To line up with the client seemed to go against everything I believed. It was taking responsibility away from the client and giving it to the therapist. It was making the client dependent on the therapist. It was not respecting the inner strength of the real self. It should be the client doing it, not the therapist doing it. I could not reconcile what I had done with the theory I held.

The aftermath

However, my supervisor supported me in lining up with the client, saying that it seemed quite legitimate to him in the particular circumstances at hand here. He reminded me of my old slogan: 'You alone can do it, but you don't have to do it alone.'

What I have moved on to is a belief that what we are talking about is not therapy, but a preliminary act of clearing the ground so that any therapy can take place at all. This makes a distinction between doing therapy and doing other things which help the therapy and in that sense are therapeutic. There are many examples of this: some people may have a very poor sense of boundaries and limits in their lives, and finishing the session on time may be therapeutic for such a person, although it is not therapy; one may ask a client to lie down to make fantasy or regression easier, and lying down may be therapeutic in this sense, but it is not therapy; I may ask clients to take off their glasses before going into an active phase of the session, but the taking off of glasses is not therapy. Similarly, siding with the client may take some of the pressure off temporarily, long enough to enable the client to muster more resources, but it is not therapy. The therapy is when the client does it on her own and for herself.

There seem to be many instances where the therapist does this kind of activity, clearing the way, or laying foundations, or offering choices which may not have been seen before by the client. They are all part of the therapeutic process, but they are all things the therapist does, rather than things the client does. And it is the things the client does which are the real therapy. This has always seemed to me a very important distinction, and now more so than ever with the new example in this case history. This was the hard-earned lesson: that even such an extreme departure from good practice could be admitted under the heading of 'foundations for therapy'. These are things which make therapy possible.

I now consider this episode to have been extremely important as a turning-point in the whole process of therapy for Sarah. Without it, I feel as if we would still be stuck with her mother, totally blocking off any other areas we might need to be working on. Her mother did in fact remain an issue for some time after this, but we found it much more possible to deal with her, and in a recent session Sarah even found herself feeling sorry for her mother.

Don't take it to heart

This example is much more brief. It concerns a middle-aged woman with a secure and well-paid job, who disassociated herself from the person who did the job. She was quite distinct from this person, whom she regarded as just a kind of automaton, often described as 'that thing', to indicate the contempt and even disgust which filled her when she thought about it. But she did not regard this attitude of her own as a problem: rather she wanted to spend her time giving accounts of how badly other people had treated her, and in particular how badly her mother had always treated her, and how justified she was in rejecting her mother.

She went abroad for an extended holiday, and on her return

described with disgust how she had put on a false face for the visit to some old friends and relatives. She criticized herself more and more vehemently for this automatic behaviour, until at last she tried to remove or destroy the false face by scratching at her own face with her nails, howling and wailing at the same time. I did not attempt to interrupt her, because in the first place it did not seem part of my useful role, and in the second place she had made it clear that any kind of physical contact would not be welcome. When the session came to an end she looked in the hall mirror on the way out, and saw that her face was bleeding in two or three places. I was deeply impressed with this scene, as it seemed to me that it was a perfect exemplification of her self-punitive attitude. Now she could not deny that she punished herself, because the physical evidence was there in those scratches.

When she returned for the next few sessions, every time she referred to someone else ill-treating her, I came back saying something like, 'Before we talk about how someone else is ill-treating you, let's go more deeply into the question of how you ill-treat yourself.' I felt very strong when doing this, as if I was in the right, and was pursuing the really essential question.

Before long, she left the therapy, saying I never listened to her, I did not take any real interest in her, she was fed up with being lectured to, what she did was her business, and I should give up being a therapist, if that was the best I could do.

Discussing this later, when I had acquired a supervisor, it became clear to me that what was wrong was my counter-transference. I had taken the incident of the face-scratching as important because it was important to me. It was my evidence, my idea, my case that I was building up. It was much more to do with me and my feelings, my reactions, my judgements, than it was to do with the client. Consequently, it felt to the client like an imposition, and like my stuff – which indeed it was.

The hard-earned lesson here was that I must not take things to heart – not let incidents or events involving the client have such an effect on me that I take them as my own. To do otherwise is to play some counter-transferential game. Before this happened I was much more prone to take my authentic experience as a good guide to what to do in therapy; now I realize that authenticity is not enough. I have to recognize that authenticity can be counter-transferential, in the sense that it can be my experience as contrasted with the client's experience. I was quite relieved at a conference recently to discover that Irving Yalom (an authority on existential therapy and group therapy), whom I would take as a therapist worthy of some respect, had a very similar experience written up in one of his books.

There is a world outside

This is a more general point, which emerged from several different sources and several different clients. I had always thought that the effects of therapy should be visible in the session itself. The whole point was to see something happening in front of one's very eyes. This is a very common feeling among therapists, and is actually enshrined in some research methods, such as, for example, that of Alvin Mahrer (1985), who writes about 'in-session outcomes' as being the basic object of worthwhile research. It can, of course, be very frustrating for a therapist to spend many hours with a client, and then not to see the important changes when they come. I remember back in the 1960s it was a common experience for analysts who had spent five years or so working with someone assiduously, to see them go to a weekend workshop and make the breakthrough which they had been prepared for.

The first of my own experiences in this area was in connection with a young man who had done some very good work in therapy, but who had got stuck. It seemed there was an important step of some kind which he had to take, but he couldn't seem to take it. We both got quite frustrated by the lack of progress.

Then he was involved in a car crash, during which he nearly died. During the crash itself, and in the operating theatre afterwards, he had some experiences which he regarded as deep and shattering. He got a completely new look at his whole life up to that point. When he recommenced therapy, there had obviously been the big breakthrough which we had been waiting for and never getting. He had gone on to a quite different place, where all the problems looked much different and much easier. Within a short time the therapy was over, and we parted with great good feelings.

The second example was again a man, nearly forty in this case, who found it extremely difficult to express any feelings. He was rather an obsessive type, who wanted to keep control of everything, and was very reluctant to do anything which might be dramatic or emotional.

During the course of the therapy, his grandmother died. It turned out she had been very good to him as a child, and had in fact mothered him much more than his actual mother. He experienced acute grief at her death, and I encouraged him to feel the feelings and express them in the session. One whole session he did nothing but cry, and in one or two other sessions he dealt with other feelings which he had about her.

The therapy took a turn for the better once this had happened, and the client seemed much better able to understand what the therapy was about and how it worked. A few months later we made a decision to end the therapy for the foreseeable future. I doubt whether this would have happened if his grandmother had not died.

The third example was on the island of Skyros, where I did some research on the way people were experiencing the growth groups there. One of the most remarkable examples was a young woman from Norway, who had been in several groups, and had not experienced anything very extraordinary in them. Then, one evening on the beach, when the sun was setting, she suddenly knew who she was and what she was about. She took coloured felt pens and covered several sheets of paper with words like, 'I am free!' 'I am me!!!' It was an important breakthrough for her, which had effects for the whole time she was there, and looked like being something permanent. I don't think the group therapist ever found out about this, and probably thought he had failed with this woman.

What these examples show, it seems to me, is that there is a world outside the therapy room. And it is often things in this world which are just as important, or more important, than what happens in the consulting room. This gives me extra humility, in the knowledge that what I am doing, whether it be stupid or brilliant, is only a small part of the experience of the client: a sobering but salutary thought.

The hard-earned lesson here is that I have to be prepared to see my work taken over by outside forces, which may make me feel quite small and ineffectual, and that that has to be all right.

Not the world saviour

When I first started as a psychotherapist I took on all comers. Partly I needed the experience, and partly I needed the money. Partly I thought that primal integration was capable, because of its flexibility, of handling all problems. But before very long, I started to come to the conclusion that there were some clients who were not for me, and whom I would do better to avoid.

One who came to me was referred by another therapist, who supposedly did not have any free time to see this man. He was very disappointed not to be seen by the first therapist, and continually found fault with what I did, and also found some quite subtle and successful ways of sabotaging the therapy. I came to the view in the end that I was unwise to take him on in the first place.

Another two – a man and a woman, no connection between them – managed to foil my every attempt to inveigle them into some other attitude than that of crushed victim. They spoke very quietly, almost inaudibly, and only wanted to talk about how bad things were for them. It didn't seem to matter whether I went along with it, or tried to explore with them another side of the matter – nothing seemed to make any difference at all. I came to the view that I was the wrong therapist for such people.

I began to be more selective about the clients I took on. I became quite good at referring someone on in a constructive and helpful way, so that they saw the point of it and accepted it.

Recently I saw somebody for an initial session and decided instantly that this was not someone I could work with in any successful way. It is important to recognize that this was due to my own weaknesses, not anything the client was doing wrong. I try to work on my own weaknesses in my own supervision, and in my own therapy.

It is very important, of course, to do this as early in the relationship as possible. The longer it is left the worse it is for the client and for the therapist. Many clients have problems with rejection, and to be rejected by someone who seemed to have the promise of helping one must be one of the worst types of rejection.

One time I left it very late was in the case of a young man who had no sexual relationship and found it hard to get in touch with his feelings. I worked with him for three years, and in that time he had met and gone out with an attractive and forceful woman for two years. One day he told me she had walked out on him. I asked him how he felt about that, and he said he felt nothing. After probing for some time to see whether this was an initial shock reaction, and discovering that it seemed to be the direct truth, I felt that if this was all the result after three years' work, he might as well try elsewhere. Obviously the work with me was to a great extent ineffectual. So I told him not to come back next week. He seemed a bit shaken, and asked if he could ever come back. I said he might come back after a year, if he then still wanted to. But he never did. I now think this was quite the wrong thing to have done, and that it was done from counter-transferential motives in that I had felt so useless and incompetent. It would have been much better to have set up a proper series of termination interviews, where the issues could have been explored in depth and in detail.

The hard-earned lesson here is that I cannot assume competence with all and sundry. This was hard because I did think at first that my approach was so flexible and so potent that it could benefit anyone at all; it was painful to discover otherwise.

Gods can come in handy

Here again there were two events which combined to teach me a lesson, rather than just one. The first of these was when a woman client had a dream involving a vulture. The vulture played a major role, and seemed to be one of the most significant features of the dream. All the client's associations with the vulture were negative, and for her it was quite a frightening dream for this reason.

It just so happened that the previous day I had been reading in Barbara Walker (1983) about Nekhbet, the vulture goddess of ancient Egypt. She was regarded as the origin of all things, and the greatest oracle in Egypt was located at her shrine in Nekhen (modern Al-Kab). She was the pre-dynastic matriarch, and the hieroglyph for 'grandmother' was the symbol of the vulture goddess with the flail of authority. The hieroglyph for 'mother' was the vulture on its own. So in ancient Egypt, and in other places too, the vulture was sacred and highly valued, a major goddess and a powerful cult figure. I found out later from Durdin-Robertson (1975) that Nekhbet was 'the mother of mothers, who hath existed from the beginning and is the creatrix of the world.' This made the dream quite different in meaning, and the client was greatly reassured and relieved. In this particular case, I am sure that the new interpretation was much closer to the truth for this client. It would not necessarily be so for another client at another time.

Another time a client had a dream about a powerful woman who was dominant and aggressive, both defeating people with words and also cutting off their heads with a sword. My client was inclined to see in this her animus, or inner male archetype, and to deplore the masculine qualities being exhibited by this woman, who seemed to her more masculine than feminine.

But this character seemed to me more like the goddess Athena, who was both powerful in reason and logic, and also warlike, inspiring heroes and going with them into battle. She was the only goddess on Olympus who wore armour. Jean Shinoda Bolen (1984) tells us that: 'Strategy, practicality and tangible results are hallmarks of her particular wisdom. Athena values rational think- ing and stands for the domination of will and intellect over instinct and nature.'

Yet Athena is a goddess, completely female, nothing masculine about her at all. She proves, like many other goddesses, that many so-called 'masculine qualities' can be true of the feminine too. The Woolgers (1990) suggest that Simone Weil is a good example of the Athena woman. So there is nothing about being female which precludes women from getting in touch with these forceful qualities and using them to the full. This idea appealed very much to my client, and meant a lot to her at this particular point in her life.

I now believe that a knowledge of mythology can be very useful when dealing with dreams, because they can enable a different light to be thrown on something, and another meaning to be extracted, which may be highly relevant and very useful to the client.

It may seem to the untutored mind that these were easy lessons, rather than hard-earned ones. I had always held the opinion that there is never just one meaning to a dream, and two, three or four or more interpretations may all be valid and useful. The point was, however, that I had always wanted these to come from the client. I used to believe it was wrong for therapists to offer interpretations of dreams. I held the view, very strongly, that the client should be the sole and sovereign authority as to the meaning of their dreams. The hard-earned lesson here was to see that this is too rigid a shibboleth, and that it is sometimes all right for the therapist to offer something, even something quite strong and powerful. The therapist does not have to pussyfoot around giving tentative thoughts or murmurs of encouragement, but can come right out and say something definite. The client can always reject it if it does not fit.

Conclusion

What I see on looking back over these lessons is that most of them have to do with giving up assumptions, sometimes quite grandiose assumptions. I suppose in a way it is best for therapists to have no assumptions, but that is easier said than done, and may in fact be quite impossible. Certainly I have found the giving up of some of my favourite assumptions a daunting business, and to find myself questioning the total efficacy of authenticity was particularly difficult for me.

One of the most interesting lessons, not included in the above because it did not quite fit with the format, was the lesson that I can know someone else's experience. It was one of the shibboleths which I grew up with in therapy, that you could not know what someone else was thinking or feeling. It even presented itself as an important philosophical insight, which to deny branded one as infantile. 'I am I, and you are you' was one way of putting it. But sometimes, when I was working with subpersonalities, I had a definite feeling that I knew someone else's subpersonality better than they did themselves. Later I met Alvin Mahrer, who eventually convinced me that it was theoretically and practically possible to enter into someone else's world so completely that one could

see certain things in it before the other person did; partly because
they were things the other person didn't want to see. Later I
discovered a whole transpersonal theory of the imaginal world
which made this idea even more acceptable. That wasn't really a
hard-earned lesson, because it crept up on me gradually, but I
think it was just as big and just as overturning as any of the ones
mentioned in the chapter proper.

References

Bolen, J. S. (1984) *Goddesses in Everywoman*. New York: Harper Colophon.
Durdin-Robertson, L. (1975) *The Goddesses of Chaldaea, Syria and Egypt*.
  Clonegal: Cesara Publications.
Mahrer. A. (1985) *Psychotherapeutic Change*. New York: Norton.
Ridgway, R. (1987) *The Unborn Child*. Aldershot: Wildwood House.
Rowan, J. (1990) *Subpersonalities: The People Inside Us*. London: Routledge.
Verny, T. (1982) *The Secret Life of the Unborn Child*. London: Sphere.
Walker, B. (1983) *The Women's Encyclopedia of Myths and Secrets*. San Francisco:
  Harper & Row.
Woolger, J. B. and R. J. (1990) *The Goddess Within*. London: Rider.

9 Robin Shohet

While thinking about this chapter, I came up with a few difficulties I would like to address. The first is – how is what I have learnt relevant to you? If my lessons have been hard earned, does this mean you, the reader, can learn them too by reading about them? Possibly, but only if you have learnt the lessons anyway, and reading is acting as more of a confirmation. Otherwise, learning intellectually could be confused with learning bodily and emotionally – knowledge as a substitute for experience.

The second difficulty I have has to do with being able to generalize learning, and this is on two accounts. First, my experience is mine; you may have had a similar experience, but there is a danger of applying learning that relates to my particular personality to you, with a different personality, just because the outward circumstances seem similar. For example, I very often do not respond to questions at the beginning of a session like, 'How are you?', or 'Did you have a good break?', or 'How many more sessions have we left this term?' There are good theoretical grounds for doing this. In Gestalt terms, behind the question is a statement. Also, anxiety is high at the beginning of the session (for both parties probably), and question-and-answer is an attempt to diffuse that, which may not be in the best interests of the work. By resisting the temptation to answer, even though it initially seems strange, the feelings that prompted the question emerge. Having said that, it suits my style of working. Moreover, I cannot say I never answer. Nor does this lesson necessarily have relevance to you, with a different style. Perhaps all we can do is question some of our assumptions.

Another difficulty I have about generalizing is an extension of the first – namely, that the learning takes place in a context, so I am different with each client, although I am sure there are many similarities, too. So a lesson I have learnt about not answering questions may be totally inappropriate with a particular client. Each situation needs to be new, although, paradoxically, you need to be very experienced (or just starting) to appreciate this. I think this is what Bion meant when he was talking of entering the session without memory, desire, or understanding. I also like the quote of the abbot who, when one of his monks complained that he was not following the rules, said, 'Obedience keeps the rules. Love knows when to break them.' This could be a licence for sloppiness, but

I think he meant the love that comes from a great self-discipline.

You may at this stage be wondering why I am writing this piece at all, and be catching some of my confusion. I think that is what I want. For if I have learnt anything, it is that I have not learnt as much as I thought I would have learnt when I started fifteen years ago. And that feels at different times wonderful and dreadful.

Behind my questions you may also have perceived some anxiety – that the danger in thinking one has learnt something may stop one from being in the moment and seeing the uniqueness of the particular situation. This does not only apply to my work, but to my life. It can lead to complacency, and arrogance, and paradoxically may stop my learning by thinking that I have learnt. Beware of the expert. What I fear is that with increasing emphasis on professionalization, people may not be so able to trust process, to stay with not knowing, because it can lead to very sticky places. Instead they may prefer to apply formulae or give responses that initially look good, but may ultimately be detrimental, like answering questions too readily (or not, because one is supposed not to).

My first learning may be that I do not know much about learning – my own and others'. And what may seem to be a mistake or good may turn out to be other than what I thought. In *Reframing*, Bandler and Grindler (1982) start by quoting a Chinese farmer who had apparent misfortune and then apparent good fortune – and each time things do not appear as they seem. He loses a horse – misfortune? A few days later the horse returns with two wild horses – good fortune? His son breaks a leg riding one – misfortune? No, there is a war, and he cannot be enlisted because of his broken leg, and so on.

Let me take a simple example from counselling to illustrate this, again focusing on beginnings. I have learnt to pay great attention to the first minute of a session. I have a very stuck session with a client. Going back over it, I realize I did not pay sufficient attention to the client telling me her daughter is not well. A very plausible beginning, but in fact, retrospectively, all is not well in *our* relationship. However, in the next session she is full of life. When she got home she realized how angry she was with me for not caring enough for her. If I'd caught the dynamic right at the beginning, would that have been as good? Who knows.

Another example. I have a client who has had a Wednesday six o'clock session for many years. He has a meeting. Could he come at eight o'clock. I have an eight o'clock client who often misses, wants to come fortnightly, and even then is not sure if he can afford it (he gambles, so money is not the real issue). I say to my six o'clock client, okay. I intend to change the eight o'clock, and forget to. I have just started the session with the eight o'clock, when the buzzer goes. It is my six o'clock client. It is after the Christmas break, so I am puzzled as I have no memory of the transaction and have not written it down. I then remember the whole conversation, but it is too late. I have to tell the six o'clock that I have made a mistake, and he leaves pretty angry. An elementary mistake had been made in agreeing to make the change, which I have compounded by forgetting. Or have I? The dynamics of me and my six o'clock client are now brought to the fore, and the next session is very clarifying for both of us. And there is a hidden bonus. The eight o'clock client obviously realizes what has happened, and confronts me about how I have given 'his' session away. Not only has he not confronted me before, but, for the first time, he claims ownership of the time. A new phase has begun.

I have focused on mistakes because I no longer know what is a mistake and what isn't, and anyway, nothing is fatal unless it suits either or both of the parties to make it so. I have seen brilliant work (my own and others) be de-skilling, and subtly or not so subtly induce dependence. The overall lesson might be that the ability to tolerate uncertainty and ambiguity is a very useful attribute, and certainty is dangerous.

Before going on to the actual lessons, I would like to give the reader some idea of my background, as this may throw some light on the choice of lessons. I grew up in a household where my father talked a lot about his own analysis, and was committed to a Freudian understanding of human nature. From the age of fourteen I knew I wanted to be a therapist of one sort or another. I took a degree in psychology, and later a teaching diploma. In my twenties I twice went to India to look for truth – the relationship between psychotherapy and spirituality has always been of great interest to me. I came back depressed, and went into therapy at about the same time as I started to work in a therapeutic community. The three-and-a-half years I spent there have formed the basis of my freelance career, teaching me about group dynamics and the context in which one-to-one work takes place.

I left the community to become freelance in 1979, and have since been seeing individuals, couples, running groups – particularly dream groups – training supervisors, and being a consultant to staff teams. I am in a peer-supervision dyad which meets every three weeks, and am currently having two-hourly sessions of a form of therapy called 'mind clearing'. I am also in a peer group which looks at our work in a much wider context, and has been the basis for examining core beliefs about therapy and the issue of accreditation. I think it is vital that as helpers we allow ourselves to be in the position of being helped and supported, and need to be reminded of the vulnerability of being a client, something I shall come back to later.

I will always make mistakes, and so will you

Fifteen years ago, I imagined that at some stage in my life I might reach wise-old-man status. This meant, in Sheldon Kopp's (1977) words, doing impeccable work, and in my terms, making no mistakes. This is: overly simplistic; unrealistic; not human; leads to a fear of taking risks; playing safe (which could be a mistake in itself); begs the question of how you know what a mistake is anyway; has an implicit fear around having to get it right; and implies there is a right way. If experience has taught me anything, it is that anything can be used constructively – even the grossest of so-called mistakes – providing there is a willingness to learn and admit fallibility. Moreover, apparent infallibility is not good for the profession. It creates an even bigger gap than already exists between counsellor and client, and leads to clients projecting their own wisdom on to the counsellor.

Here is an example of a series of mistakes from a session of many years ago which still causes me some embarrassment. I had been seeing X for about a year when he came in looking distressed, saying there was a taxi downstairs that needed paying. I didn't immediately realize what he wanted, which was for me to pay the taxi. He said he had just been robbed, and rather than miss the session altogether, he wanted to come, but he didn't have a penny. My first possible mistake was to pay for the taxi, thinking the poor man has just been robbed, and how committed he was to have come. Then the story unfolded.

Before coming to counselling he had gone with a group of friends to a strip club and had been robbed there of about sixty pounds, of which twenty was to pay for the session. He now wanted me to give him forty pounds to take home. He would then give me a cheque next week for two sessions – plus the loan of forty, plus the taxi fare. I believed he would, but obviously refused. He upped the stakes: I was threatening his marriage; he could not go home without the money – what story could he tell his wife? If he said he had been robbed, she would have wanted to know why he hadn't told the police. His whole secret would come out if I didn't give him forty pounds. His marriage would be ruined, and it would be my fault.

My counsellor-part said to myself, you must be joking. But some other part of me was finding the pressure hard to resist. Knowing that my 'internal supervisor' was not working, in desperation I asked him to go into another room while I phoned my external supervisor. A few words from her were enough to bring me out of my trance, and I came back and said I would not give him the money. He said how disappointed he was. He thought I was more than just a counsellor who played it by the book, someone who cared enough to save his marriage. The following week he came back and said I had been right to refuse.

Where in this is the hard-earned lesson? If I examine my discomfort, I realize that when a part of myself is touched that has not been worked through, call it pathology, then clients will unerringly know this and use it when necessary and here is where the mistakes happen. What struck me about the above incident in retrospect was how collusive the relationship must have been *before* the incident for him to have even dared ask for the money. And even though I knew enough not to give it to him outright, emotionally I was still ripe for blackmail. Just for the record, what had been touched off was something like this: I identified with him in that something grossly unfair had happened to him in being robbed. Sure, he set it up by going to the strip club, but he did not expect to be robbed. When something goes wrong for *me*, I expect the world to make it up to me, so, of course, I felt I should make it better for him as well. Also, as I fear being destructive, the threat of destroying a marriage was a way of also getting to me.

I will always have blind spots, I will never be immune from such errors. I sometimes wonder if in some ways the more aware I supposedly am, the more prone to blind spots I become. This leads me to my second lesson.

I am always less aware and open than I think

If the above example shows the possibility of gross error, it also came as a shock to my ideas of self-awareness. This image of myself as an aware person, reinforced by supervision and therapy, is, I fear, an illusion, most frequently corrected by a confrontative partner, but never really let go of. I rediscovered this quite strongly recently.

I like to think of myself as reasonably open, and certainly open to challenge by my clients, who have on occasions been extremely confrontative. About a year ago I was helping to organize a conference on accreditation. I realized that one of the things accreditation can do is to make the 'accreditee' put forward only his or her strengths, and hide their weaknesses in order to be accredited. Is it okay to put on an application form, 'sometimes I resent my clients; want to go to bed with them; am bored, etc.'? Yet it happens to everyone I have talked to. So I made a suggestion that we try a mock accreditation procedure, whereby I had to convince the panel how *bad* I was, and they had to find the best in me. To pass, I would have to convince them of my faults. I started a little tentatively, feeling quite vulnerable: 'I take long holidays.' Reply: 'Well, that teaches your clients not to be dependent.' 'I yawn in sessions.' 'Well, you are giving your clients an opportunity to confront you, and give you immediate feedback that other counsellors might repress.' I warmed up to the game and decided to commit myself: 'I'm sloppy about keeping to fixed times – I run courses, so I can't guarantee a set time for someone in the way the analysts do.' 'Well, that teaches your clients not to live in a fools' paradise', etc.

The following week an interesting thing happened. A client who had said she had initially minded the summer break, but in fact after a while had felt really good that she was not dependent on counselling, suddenly launched into a tirade about my long summer breaks. Another started to tell me how lazy I was in not giving enough notice of my courses. Another challenged me on my yawning for the first time. No less than six clients confronted me that week on themes brought up in the mock accreditation procedure. It was as if they could see that I had tackled one or two issues in a way that I had not before and were saying, 'Now I guess you can take this. I couldn't tell you before.'

From supervision I know that facing my own blocks helps the client move on, so I am not unused to this experience. But there was something a bit different here. It was as if I had allowed the world to know more about my real weaknesses, and it was now okay for them to be commented on explicitly. How much more is there to go, I wonder. I advise everyone to try this 'reverse accreditation' procedure. As Alan Watts (1974) says:

> I have always been fascinated by the law of reversed effort. Sometimes I call it the backwards law. When you try to stay on the surface of the water, you sink; but when you try to sink you float. When you hold your breath you lose it – which immediately calls to mind an ancient and much neglected saying: 'Whosoever would save his soul shall lose it'.

I sometimes wonder if the whole business of getting to know oneself is just an illusion. A blind spot is by definition blind, and the more I think I know the more prone to illusion I can get. I believe that understanding oneself is important, but perhaps the self-knowledge is just a very subtle way of being in control. In my case, I think I tried to understand as a way of coping with my father's analysis. As such, self-awareness and well-developed intuition are in themselves defences, as well as being very useful. I shall return to the question of illusion later.

Over the last few years I have been part of an improvisation drama group, which has taught me as much about being in the here and now (being aware) as counselling and therapy. For the drama to work, both parties have to be exquisitely sensitive to each other, rather than merely concentrating on their own performance. Keith Johnstone (1981) talks about accepting offers the other person has made. (An example of an offer could be someone walking into a room and saying, 'Smith, isn't it?' If the other person says, 'No, it isn't' they have probably blocked, whereas if he says something like, 'My God, after all these years', he has accepted the offer, and given an opportunity for the drama to develop.) He found that those who had a great need for control regularly blocked the other person, for example by trying to make the other person follow their ideas, and that this blocking was a hostile act. He realized this because when he told people to love each other they no longer blocked. The relevance of this is that I did not realize how much I blocked others. This was very salutary for me because the role of counsellor can encourage all sorts of blocking, like not answering questions immediately. I like the idea quoted in Sheldon Kopp's book (1977) where he writes: 'Over the years, again and again, young therapists have come to me for supervision complaining: "I'm stuck. For a while the work was going well, but now we're at an impasse . . . My patient is blocking and I can't seem to get him over his (or her) resistance."' At times like these, says Kopp, it's difficult for the therapists to understand that a 'therapeutic impasse' is simply a time when the therapist is trying to make a patient do something that the patient is not ready to do. He goes on to say:

> Where the traditional concept of 'resistance' is primary in the thinking of the therapist, it is the patient who is seen as responsible for anything that goes wrong. It makes more sense to me to reserve the term 'resistance' for those sane, creative, realistically self-protective attitudes and behaviours the patient uses to cope with the errors perpetrated by the therapist.

The hidden power struggle is my next lesson.

Therapists have a lot of power, and I like this more than I like to admit

I was talking to my partner about this, and she said, 'You know, the accurate intuition you have gives you a lot of power.' She paused and then added, 'No, it's not the intuition itself. I can imagine the way you use it gives the client very little space sometimes and puts them in a double-bind, because your acute intuition is the very reason they have come to you.' I did not like this, but knew there was truth in what she was saying, so I asked her to develop the theme. 'Well, I think you are quite attached to being right, and so if something did not feel right to me as the client, I might go along with you and not challenge you for a variety of reasons. One is that you might stop sharing your intuitions; two, you might be right and I could be blocking; and, three, I don't know if you know how convincing you can be, and need to be.'

After she had said this I was reminded of something in Guggenbuhl-Craig's book (1982):

> . . . whenever something must be imposed by force, the conscious and unconscious motives of those involved are many faceted. An uncanny lust for power lurks in the background . . . Quite frequently, the issue at stake appears to be not the welfare of the protected, but the power of the protector.

He was referring to the power of social workers to impose care orders, and so on, but he could be talking of the power of insight and interpretation. I see it sometimes when a client feeds back a remark I think I have just made in passing – as if there was any such thing – and he or she has said what an impact it has had. I find it hard to accept the lesson of my power for two reasons: one is that I don't want to recognize how important I am for my clients. Because of a fear of my own dependence, I am reluctant to make anyone important for me, and therefore block out my own importance for others; the second is, as my partner pointed out, I like the power my intuition gives me more than I care to acknowledge. I believe that transference of one sort or another is always there, but I invoke it in a particular way with my insight – an all-knowing parent. And now I make the connection that that is the game my father played.

In the introduction I quoted my way of managing questions at the beginning of a session. There would appear to be sound therapeutic reasons for such non-responses. And yet I cannot altogether be sure there isn't a power element in this too. I sometimes like being able to be where the client isn't, and my uncomfortableness in writing this confirms the truth of it as I rush inside my head to qualify and explain.

Here is an example around using intuition as a source of power. A man comes to see me, referred by a colleague who has had to stop seeing him because he is leaving the area. My colleague had originally been seeing the client and his wife, but the client, or more accurately his drinking, had been identified as the source of the problem in the marriage. I listen to his story. They have very little sex, and he works long hours away from home. After a few minutes, my first intervention is to say, 'Why do you need to punish your wife so much?' This plainly shocks him, as he has not seen himself as aggressive in his actions – more needing support for tendencies (drink, loss of libido) or demands (work) that are beyond his control. In fact, the intervention turns out to be useful in opening up a whole new area of work. However, the manner and timing of the intervention had an edge which owed something to competitive feelings with my colleague over what I thought was a collusion in his work with the client.

I am slow to learn this lesson about my need for power. I remember it best from being a client, and realizing how sensitive I was to every gesture of the therapist. I noticed as a client how much I held back, especially in groups. And so regularly each year I put myself in a position of not knowing, of being stuck and lost, usually by going to a workshop or a meditation that stretches me. At these times clients report a softness in me, and more humility and understanding of their shame and resistances.

My job is to manage the counselling framework, not the client's life

The idea for this lesson came from Sheldon Kopp (1977), who writes:

> . . . the therapist is helped to feel comfortable simply by being in charge of the therapy, leaving the patient to be in charge of his or her own life. It is only then that the therapist can offer the expert services of a professional guide, and so avoid the impasse born of the presumption of thinking that the therapist knows what is best for the patient. By concentrating on the therapeutic work, the therapist gets unstuck, leaving the patient free to discover what he or she wants out of life, how to go about getting it, and at what cost. It is the patient who must choose just how he or she is to live. When the therapist helps the patient to be happier without needing the patient to change, the therapist's own impeccable work will be reward enough.

I once had a client who was doing research into her family history, and would update me in her sessions about the latest developments. In one session I 'helpfully' made a suggestion as to how to proceed with the research, based on my own experiences of tracing my family history. She seemed very pleased as she had not thought of this particular approach before. However, in the next session she seemed withdrawn, although a lot of progress in looking through records had been made in the intervening week. I suspected that I had been over-involved and asked her if her mood had had anything to do with the last session. She was able to tell me that I had robbed her of making her own discoveries, just like her older brother had done. This experience, and other similar ones, helped me to realize how much I wanted to manage people's lives. From time to time I notice I am still tempted. It invariably means there is something of my own that I need to attend to.

I have more need of my clients than I think

Recently, I saw someone for a one-off session. I had known her from other contexts both as a member of a group I had facilitated and as a peer. She had really wanted the session to sort out some career difficulties. I fitted her in, and was perhaps a little resentful at her persistence. At the end of the session, she asked me how much I charged. When I told her, she said, 'You're bloody expensive.' She realized I didn't like that, and after the session I noticed I couldn't let it go. I rationalized the reasons: she knows several people I know and would bad-mouth me, etc. (projection of my anger), but I was puzzled as it was not such a terrible statement.

And then I realized I had allowed myself to be caught because I had wanted something from her – recognition of how I had put myself out. And part of why I enjoy myself so much as a counsellor is that on the whole I want less from my clients than in other relationships; but more often than I think, I am wanting something. The paradox is that the more vulnerable I allow myself to be (e.g., by acknowledging my needs), the better the counselling. By denying my needs, I am not only out of touch with myself, but let the client carry the neediness for both of us.

The lesson first appeared to me when working in the Richmond Fellowship, when I realized how hurt I was when my counsellees, with whom I had a special relationship, would attack me in the community meeting, and how much narcissism I had. Wanting something is not in itself bad if it is recognized; it is when I do not acknowledge my own need of my clients that I can get punitive.

The work and the role of counselling offer me a way of being that I sometimes strive for in my everyday life. I am involved, mostly quite caring, can use my intuition, take risks, and share certain parts of myself where I think appropriate. I have a framework which enables me to understand certain aspects of the relationship, and comment on them non-judgementally so that even if attacked I can understand it and not be as reactive as I am in my everyday life. Because the work is so rewarding, there are times when I work to feel better. Initially, the work goes well (have you ever noticed that when feeling bad you can work well?). Ultimately, however, this compensatory neediness of clients is not congruent, and leads to burn-out. At times like this I have to examine my support systems very carefully.

Finally, all my life I have thought that insight will protect me from my needs – so that understanding the dynamics of the counselling relationship will help me not to feel so vulnerable to clients. This is a defence that I adopted early, and now realize does not work. If I pay very careful attention, I can sometimes mind dreadfully about some things that clients say. I notice it in my body. I very quickly compensate with understanding, but this takes its toll. When I have been able to acknowledge my vulnerability to myself I have felt calmer, and have had less need to distance myself from clients.

Conclusion

As I was writing this, I tried to link all these disparate lessons. What struck me, and in a way this could be called a sixth lesson, is that one of the most important ingredients in a counsellor's toolbox is an appreciation of paradox. A mistake might not be a mistake; the more I try to be aware the blinder I become; the more I try to deny my power the more ways it will leak out subtly; the more I try to be helpful to my clients the less effective I am; the more I deny my needs the more I will use my clients to satisfy those needs.

Earlier I mentioned the law of reversed effort. In training people to be counsellors, I give a session on being very bad counsellors. It is invariably very liberating, and unexpectedly counsellees report having good sessions. Giving permission to be bad can make one good – trying to be good can be destructive. Perhaps by its very nature it is not possible to learn about paradox, because as soon as you think you have understood, you haven't.

I wanted to take this idea of paradox further by looking at the relationship between counselling and spirituality, which has interested me for over twenty years, since before my first trip to India in 1971. I have included it because the relationship between psyche, soul, truth, consciousness – whatever words one chooses to use – is one that has in different ways underpinned my practice, and one that I am increasingly willing to talk about with clients. In terms of lessons, it is probably the hardest and perhaps the only lesson really worth learning. If the major spiritual traditions are right, and I believe they are, then all our misery is based on a false notion of who we are, rather than uncovering traumas from the past.

Before 1968 I was very much into the Freudian idea of God being a projection of the father, and the whole idea of religion seemed very escapist. I then had a near-psychotic experience when taking dope, which resulted in my seeing the unity of all things, that love forms the basis of all relationships, and that at a very deep level we create our own realities. Psychology gave way to a study of Eastern religion, practising meditation, and an eventual trip to India. I came back quite depressed after trying to renew a very destructive relationship, and realized I had some basic sorting out to do. Far from psychology being an escape, my flight to India was in fact the escape. I committed myself to psychotherapy, and would not even talk about spirituality.

Now the wheel has turned again, and I struggle to combine the world of counselling and psychotherapy and the world of spirituality. Sometimes I think they can be combined by being fully in the present. Sometimes I think that even the deepest psychological insights pale in comparison with spiritual truths which shake us out of the illusion of separateness.

The loss of this illusion of being a separate ego has been described in glowing terms by John Wren-Lewis (1991) after a near death experience: 'I now know exactly why the Book of Genesis says that God looked upon *all* He had made – not just beautiful sunsets, but dreary hospital rooms and traumatized sixty-year-old bodies – and saw that it was very good.' And continues:

> What I am trying to describe is no vague feeling of 'good to be alive'. On the contrary, I no longer cared if John lived or ceased to be altogether . . . This is in no sense a high from which I can come down. The sense of awe-ful wonder has at the same time feeling of utter obviousness and ordinariness . . . From this perspective, the term *altered* state of consciousness would be a complete misnomer, for the state is one of simple normality. It seems, rather, as if my earlier state, so called 'ordinary' human consciousness, represents the real alteration – a deviation from the plain norm, a kind of artificially blinkered or clouded condition where the bodymind has the absurd illusion that it is somehow a separate individual entity over against everything else.

It is this 'bodymind' we take to counselling to be fixed, and what

Wren-Lewis is suggesting is that the whole premise of an 'I' to be counselled or an 'I' as a counsellor may be erroneous. We are again in the territory of paradox. For on one level the experiences of Wren-Lewis and others may seem to undermine the basis of counselling; on another level I experience the work of counselling as the best I can do. Either way the process of being able to share some of my doubts, uncertainties, mistakes, and beliefs in these hard-earned lessons has in itself been a lesson for me, which I hope will have some relevance to you.

References

Bandler, R. and Grindler, J. (1982) *Reframing*. Utah: Real People Press.
Guggenbuhl-Craig, A. (1982) *Power in the Helping Professions*. Dallas: Spring.
Johnstone, K. (1981) *Impro*. London: Methuen.
Kopp, S. (1977) *Back to One*. Palo Alto: Science and Behaviour Books.
Watts, A. (1974) *The Wisdom of Insecurity*. London: Rider.
Wren-Lewis, J. A. (1991) A Reluctant Mystic, *Self and Society*, 19(2).

10   Moira Walker

It is never easy to write a brief biography, but it has made me question how I have arrived in my present job of running a university counselling service. It seems a long way from where I started, and the journey has been a mixture of historical accident, positive decisions, and, at one stage, taking any vaguely relevant job that fitted with caring for young children. Consequently, my background is mixed – for many years I was employed on short-term contracts, and was balancing two or three part-time jobs simultaneously.

Initially, after graduating, I worked with children and families, a time I value enormously as a backdrop to all my subsequent work. I qualified as a social worker, and worked in psychiatric settings before moving back into family work. This marked the beginning of my interest in abuse, which has grown through the years. There followed a period of several years when I both taught, primarily in social policy, and continued in practice in a range of settings, both voluntary and statutory, in hospitals, and in the community. Although these years can be viewed with suspicion on my c.v. by those who prefer to see a traditional career pattern, I value the richness of the experience I gained at that time.

My first counselling post was a surprise to me. I wanted it, but had no expectation of being appointed. That was the first surprise. The second was the nature of the work. As I explain later, it was considerably more demanding than I expected. I had wanted the chance to do more in-depth and ongoing therapeutic work. It certainly provided that. At this stage I was still teaching both in a polytechnic and for the Open University – throughout my career both academic and clinical work have been very important to me. But my interest in the clinical work grew, as did my desire to develop my knowledge and skills. I wanted to undertake further training, and was accepted on to the Warwick University psychotherapy course. That was a very important step in many ways, and the course continued to be significant for many years. After completing as a student, I returned with a different hat and became a clinical supervisor for the course.

I have now been involved in counselling for twelve years, the last seven in the same place. As I write I am amazed to note that I have stayed that long, but glad that I have. Summing yourself up briefly in terms of orientation is horribly difficult, but some things are sufficiently important not to be omitted. I am a feminist counsellor, although there is no space here to explain my meaning, except to say that for me it essentially incorporates political and structural understandings. Although I am very concerned to understand the interface between various theoretical approaches, and would want to be open to utilizing aspects of many, nevertheless, it is the psychodynamic school that I am most drawn to, and find most helpful, challenging, and exciting.

Ring me whenever you need to

Counselling inevitably brings the counsellor into contact with a level of human misery and suffering that is avoided by most of the population. Particularly for the relatively new counsellor this can evoke a desire to rescue the client, to quickly make him/her feel better, and take away their pain. It is hard to acknowledge that rescuing is not possible, and that pain is both inevitable, and an unavoidable component of the route to resolution. As experience and knowledge are consolidated, it is easier to appreciate more fully that the client has to discover his/her own route out of the mire; that the agony has to be encountered, not avoided; and that the journey can be arduous and sometimes lengthy, though often deeply satisfying and worthwhile.

However, recognizing that rescue is not possible, and quick solutions not generally available, may be learnt the hard way. There are pitfalls along the road towards this recognition that are not always possible to avoid in the early stages of being a counsellor. Meeting with distressed and distressing clients is never straightforward, and is particularly powerful when first experienced. Within this context both participants in the counselling process may feel that the hour or two a week on offer is woefully insufficient, and that it cannot meet the needs that are painfully evident, and often vividly expressed. The consequent resulting feelings of anxiety and inadequacy engendered in the counsellor lead to the risk of the ring-me-whenever-you-need-to scenario.

Clearly, any suggestion of total availability is highly risky. I doubt if there are any counsellors and therapists who are genuinely able to be therapeutic twenty-four hours a day over any length of time. The majority, both for their own self-protection, and for their clients, need to impose clear limits. As I write this now it seems painfully obvious that this is the case, but that was not always so.

Although I hope I have never allowed myself to feel exactly indispensable, I have certainly experienced a sense of inadequacy that what I was offering was so insufficient that the only possible response was to become more available and accessible to the client. To say now that this was not helpful and that I was forced to reconsider my own actions is best illustrated and demonstrated by an example.

I had offered a telephone number and between-session contact in response to a particularly distressed client, who had already acted out in somewhat dramatic ways. He felt he could not manage between appointments without contacting me. He expressed that need very powerfully. My response to this, although apparently an attempt to meet his need, was not only a mistake but entirely inappropriate and unhelpful.

I failed to recognize that at the time, but to explain the point I will expand further. It is in the context of a situation familiar to many readers and counsellors. They will recognize the balancing act of living with both young children and a demanding job, and know it is never easy. Consider then, this situation. It is two o'clock in the morning. You have just fallen asleep with your measles-ridden small child beside you. The telephone rings. You are rudely awakened, as is your child, who protests loudly. You, too, would like to protest in a similar vein, but the distress of your child is matched by the distress of your client on the other end of the telephone.

In such circumstances it is impossible to respond in a therapeutic, or even vaguely useful, manner. It transpired that I had unintentionally offered what I could not give. I had acted with good intentions but poor judgement. It was most unhelpful to the client, severely deprived and damaged as a child, to be faced with the undeniable evidence of competition for attention from the counsellor's own child. It was not easy to acknowledge that it was my own actions that had resulted in this early-morning débâcle, but it was certainly a significant learning experience.

I learnt the hard way that this client, and others who presented similarly, could be worked with differently and more effectively. I learnt only to offer what I could give, generously and with certainty, and I learnt the value of working within designated boundaries. One lesson was that secure and predictable boundaries operate as a powerful psychological holding agent. Although it seems obvious to me now, I had not then recognized the anxiety aroused in clients by an anxious counsellor, and that the counsellor needs to acknowledge and appropriately deal with such feelings, and not be rushed into responses.

The consequences for my own practice of this and similar situations was that I no longer easily invited contact between sessions. On occasions when I was tempted to do so, I would carefully consider both my own motivation and the probable consequences both for myself and the client. As a result I became very much clearer in what I could offer, and took the greatest care to be reliable, trustworthy, and constant. I also became very aware of the consequences of any unavoidable lapses within this framework, and of the necessity of acknowledging and working with these. Over the years my client load has become progressively more complex, and yet I have found this stance to be generally facilitative. It is also both protective towards myself, while offering a helpful model to clients. It was a lesson hard learnt, but thereafter valuably applied.

There is an inevitable danger of swinging from one end of the pendulum to the other – the once-bitten-twice-shy syndrome. So I continue to be flexible rather than rigid; to consider when it is helpful to make exceptions, and when more time or extra contact will be therapeutic and not anti-therapeutic. The central and essential element of that hard-learnt lesson can be summarized in the following way that others may find useful.

Always stop, think, and rigorously ask yourself these questions: if this client really needs more time and cannot cope without, can s/he be worked with within this context, or should I consider referral to another agency that offers more time and support? Am I missing something and therefore not working effectively within the time I do have? If so, more contact will be simply more of the same until the difficulty is identified. Is the client really telling me that it feels that nothing and no one is sufficient, and that the pain seems too great? If so, offering a little extra time is a palliative that avoids the client's experience. Or am I attempting to dismiss my anxieties rather than consider them?

It may be that the client is, for example, encountering particular traumas or difficulties, and s/he may need more time or greater access than was initially agreed. You may therefore feel it would be appropriate to offer more, but great care should still be exercised. It is here that a second stage of the lesson comes into play, a key factor being the involvement of the client in the decision: is it possible to agree with him/her for how long the extra sessions will continue? (Remembering that many counsellors and services are under enormous pressure, and cannot realistically offer two- or three-times weekly in an open-ended way.) How will the client feel when the original pattern of meetings is resumed? If an out-of-hours telephone number is given, how will s/he react if the counsellor is not there, or is not able to talk at that time? The counsellor needs to consider how the overall process of counselling will be affected: for instance, in the example above, how will the

obvious presence of the counsellor's children be received and interpreted?

Asking these questions does not mean that boundaries should
not be adjusted or moved. It does suggest that doing so is a
considered therapeutic move that has its own implications. A
casual, ill-considered response is either careless practice, or reflects
the counsellor's own needs and anxieties. To sum up, I not infre-
quently have feelings of inadequacy, but I have learnt not to
indulge this with an ill-considered response of apparent generosity
of the just-ring-me-when-you-need-to variety. It does not work.

And some for me too, please

However complex and intertwined the motives of those entering
counselling – and it is obviously important to recognize for
yourself what it is about for you – it demands considerable
resources of resilience and energy. As clients feel stronger, so they
leave and take their new-found strength into the wider world, but
another takes their place; the demand for counselling is constant,
and the needs of the client considerable.

New to the work, with a naïve but incorrect conviction this was
a soft option to my previous post in a desperately overworked and
under-resourced social work team, I was in danger of becoming
submerged by the sheer number of clients I was seeing. I
recognized in myself, not inaccurately, an ability to work well and
energetically under pressure, but did not so quickly learn that this
did not preclude the need for limits to be set and maintained. I
suspect that I even naïvely believed that those managerially responsible would be concerned with my well-being. It was not so.

Simply put, the more clients I saw, the happier they were. As
time went on I learnt, as I became progressively more tired, that
the only person who was going to take responsibility for ensuring
a reasonable workload was myself; and that this involved saying
no, often. Unfortunately, it could not only be said the once; the
message had to be repeated. Such repetitions may feel parrot-like,
but they are necessary. Pressures to take more work and absorb
more clients come from all directions, or so it may seem. For
instance, saying no to distressed potential clients, while already
working under the pressure of an existing caseload is hard. Some
readers may work in environments that are protective: they may
have a senior colleague or manager who acts as a buffer zone, and
who holds a waiting list. Others are themselves the buffer, or work
alone, or in a system that is not supportive. Learning to say no,
to establish limits for yourself, and, if necessary, to argue for these

for yourself and colleagues, is not only justifiable, it is essential. Similarly, incorporating time and space for reflection, reading, and creating and utilizing a support system is not an optional extra or a personal indulgence, but a vital aspect of effective counselling.

Telling clients they have to wait is difficult, but so is resisting pressure to increase caseloads that come from others – for instance, colleagues and workers from other agencies, and senior staff in employing institutions. However, it is equally important to do so, although problematic, particularly if they have actual power and ultimate control over resource distribution.

It helps to identify and recognize that tactics aimed at persuading the counsellor to take on more can be utilized. Some of the persuaders are genuinely and deeply concerned about the client, others want to shift the problem, relieve their own anxiety, or extricate themselves from responsibility. Different strategies create different dilemmas for the counsellor; for example, there are variations on the theme of, 'you're really the only person in the area with the skills to help this one'. It is a powerful tactic – but beware of flatterers. Acknowledge and value your own skill; do not devalue your expertise, but perceiving yourself as either unique or irreplaceable is misplaced and dangerous. Another tactic relates to possible suicide risks, inevitably touching an anxiety in most of us (this issue is discussed further below), or those who present with a major and immediate trauma or crisis. Cries of 'this one can't wait'; or 'if s/he's not seen quickly there's a real risk of suicide' have to be taken seriously. But make your own assessment. Do not become drawn in to the anxiety, panic, and dramas of others. A calm response has a calming effect, and facilitates a balanced and careful response. Some people cannot wait and do need rapid attention. Many more can and do wait, or are able to do so after an initial meeting that offers hope of future, albeit not immediate, help. Learn to pause, think, and consider – and to trust your own self.

Within this context of a potentially and often actually stressful job I have had to learn that although I have considerable energy, I cannot be an inexhaustible supply of care. There are limits, and I am exhaustible. I timetable my work with care, allowing space for the unpredictable, and the genuine and real emergencies. Inevitably there are occasions when the system slips, but it is easier to re-establish when there is a clear line to measure against, and move back towards. I encourage colleagues to do the same, and we act as a check to one another. If an ethos is agreed and established within a group of colleagues, it is easier to maintain, and becomes established as thought-out policy, rather than individual idiosyncrasy.

This lesson has been learnt within the recognition that the need for counselling cannot be entirely satisfied; the problem of demand outstripping resources is a reality, and is likely to remain so. I have also recognized that if exhaustion and overload are avoided I am left with sufficient energy and enthusiasm to consider this dilemma creatively, and have time to respond accordingly. Consequently, in my present post we currently manage to keep waiting lists short, as various schemes to prevent this have been utilized. Their planning and implementation takes time, but is a valuable investment.

It may seem obvious to suggest that avoiding exhaustion and limiting workloads really is essential, but while obvious, it does not seem an easy stance for counsellors to maintain. Some time ago I undertook a research project that examined both client and counsellor perceptions of the counselling process. Although based on a standard questionnaire, I also included space for clients to include comments on other areas not covered. Clients frequently commented that their counsellor appeared tired – whether or not this accurately reflected the counsellor's experience could not clarified, but it is an interesting observation. Clearly, tired counsellors are unlikely to function at their best, and both s/he and the client are getting less than they deserve.

Caring for ourselves is important. Acknowledging our own needs, and looking for ways of meeting them, is crucial for ourselves, our clients, and for the counselling process. As our clients deserve respect, care, attention and time, so do we. Counsellors are not a bottomless pit of loving care, and they need to acknowledge this, and ensure they have enough for themselves too. Neither should they be used as psychological dustbins by employing agencies. They are not a handy receptacle for unwanted problems, but a skilled and valuable resource.

'At-risk' clients: it can go wrong, but don't stop trying

Some counsellors will be more familiar than others with the anxieties and difficulties associated with suicidal clients. The setting you work in, and your own areas of interest will partly dictate the likelihood of encountering and working with potential suicide. Some might feel that where this is a considerable risk it implies unsuitability for counselling; others might feel the opposite – that an urgent need is being indicated that s/he would wish to respond to. Sometimes a history of serious attempts is known, but in other instances the likelihood of suicide cannot be predicted, and counselling is well under way before this is either identified by the counsellor or communicated by the client. Referral to another professional or agency may be indicated at that stage, but this is not always either appropriate, possible, or acceptable to the client. So, for a variety of reasons, both intentional and reasoned, or accidental and unintentioned, counsellors find themselves faced with the possibility of a client suicide. On some occasions this possibility becomes a reality, and it is a harsh one.

I had been working as a counsellor for some years before this happened to me. In previous jobs in the mental health field, I had inevitably encountered suicide. I was, I suspect, more familiar with this, and less anxious about the possibility, than many of my counselling colleagues. In my counselling career I had worked with several very vulnerable clients: at different times two had narrowly avoided death after very serious attempts. One had collapsed outside my office. She had taken a massive and potentially lethal overdose. She wished to die, but clearly a part of her wanted to live. Swift and skilled medical intervention saved her after a nightmarish race to hospital. Ultimately, the part of her that desired life became stronger than her wish for death (and through that, retribution on those who had damaged her, as she saw it). Her desire to die was understandable: an appalling catalogue of abuse in childhood; and in her young adult years rape by an older and trusted man, and the suicide of her partner. In time, after very intensive work with her, she began to feel stronger. She survived remarkably well. But for a while it felt as if her life hung in the balance, and staying with her, and not becoming either distanced or overwhelmed by her despair, was not easy.

That client came through the agony and despair to a point at which she wanted to live. I heard from her for many years – she is one of those people I feel privileged to have worked with, and I never cease to be amazed by her tenacity and strength. For another client it was, sadly, another ending. I worked with her for over four years. She too had been abused, and she desperately struggled to come to terms with the degradation and damage that had resulted. I struggled too. Every ounce of therapeutic skill that I possessed, I tried to use. I worked with her depression, her enormous rage, and her destructiveness to her self and all those around her. There were times when it felt as if we had turned a corner, and for a while her hopefulness outweighed her desperation. But it never lasted: if we turned a corner into smoother times, it would be followed by even greater storms.

There were many suicide attempts throughout the time I knew her. Inevitably, the number of professionals involved escalated, although it was always agreed that I should continue working with her. There seemed a general assumption, correct as it transpired, that she would eventually kill herself. Those who knew her best, and cared most – both professionally and personally – felt that the only hope for healing and recovery was in staying near her; in contacting and working with the raw pain, the despair, and the anguish. Hope lay in offering her a quality of relationship that she had never had. In the circumstances there could have been a temptation to remove myself to a safer and more impenetrable distance. It would have offered me more protection, but would not have offered her hope – although that finally proved insufficient.

In a session shortly before her death, she was calm and communicative. She described vividly how she felt she had come to a crossroads between life and death. Her imagery was powerful, her words moving, and there was a very real closeness between us. She was moving towards a decision. For me, it was a difficult session. The decision must be her own and yet I did not want her to die. She had so much potential. On happier days her sense of humour was a delight – she had a sharp wit with a touch of irony that I found immensely enjoyable. She was bright, aware, with a strong sense of justice. I liked her very much. But in the end what she had could not outweigh what she felt had been destroyed. The day before she killed herself she rang me. I could not have recognized it as such at the time, but it was a goodbye. The manner of her death was unmistakably definite: there was no possibility of survival.

When I learnt she had died I felt ill. For days I felt cold and very alone. I was not surprised, but I was deeply shocked and distressed to an extent I could not have predicted. Even writing about it, many years on, I know exactly how I felt then, and can still feel the pain. The questions I asked myself were inevitable: did I do enough? Should I have done things differently? Could someone else have done more? They are, of course, unanswerable. What I know, and knew then, is that I did all I could.

A lesson I could have learnt from this experience might have been a simple one: do not work with suicidal clients. If suicide occurs the pain is great, and giving a lot of yourself can mean losing a lot too. But this was not the case. I learnt that I survived the pain, that I was not destroyed, although I was hurt. I learnt considerably from how others responded to me at the time. Those who distanced themselves from my pain; who attempted to rationalize, diminish, or ignore my feelings, or who clearly were alarmed by them, were no help. I was left feeling alienated and alone. Those who were helpful, and I remain grateful to them, were those who were available, not worried by my pain, and who stayed with me while I was in it. What was helpful to me is also helpful to others. It reinforced for me the value of not despairing with, or giving up hope for clients, but remaining near them in their unhappiness. Clearly, that is often not sufficient, but it is certainly a necessary step in the therapeutic process. And so, I continue to work with some clients who are suicidal. I have learnt not to give up on people, although I will never forget that client.

The experts aren't always right

I was recently aware, when discussing a client with my supervisor, of a great desire for him not only to know the answer to the dilemma I had presented, but to quickly and simply tell me what it was. I felt entirely stuck with this client, and started to feel equally frustrated by my supervisor, and he with me. Rationally and sensibly, I knew an easy answer to be impossible, but it did not prevent the desire for one sneaking in. We began to unravel what this might all be about, but it reminded me of how counsellors can fall into the trap of seeking and needing 'expert' opinion.

Undoubtedly the knowledge and expertise of other practitioners, writers, and researchers can be both helpful and illuminating. There is little point in continually re-inventing the wheel when others know how it is done. Sharing knowledge, experience, and thoughts in a generous and open way allows counsellors to challenge and expand their own ideas. This is stimulating and informative, but there are dangers in believing that someone else has the answers – and even greater danger in believing you are the one with them. Perhaps we are all most susceptible in our need for answers when we are new to counselling, and most convinced by those who appear certain and confident. Personally, I am more convinced by tentativeness and questioning than by assurance and answers, particularly when the degree of assurance is not backed up by considerable clinical experience. There are those who are effective and persuasive writers or teachers, but lack the essential and crucial element of ongoing practice.

An example of my own over-zealous application of a technique came early in my counselling career after attending a workshop, and reading the relevant book. I cannot now remember the author, but the subject was 'Not asking questions in counselling'. It may have been expressed in a somewhat more sophisticated fashion, but that was the essence. The virtues of never asking questions except when absolutely necessary were firmly extolled.

I spent the next week in increasingly anti-therapeutic tangles, vainly trying to puzzle out the definition of 'absolute necessity', and not asking questions unless it was one. I began to feel increasingly like a particularly unintelligent parrot. The result was a confused and rather weary counsellor, and somewhat perplexed clients. The lesson I learnt was that while techniques have their value, they should not smother the counsellor's own self. They are a helpful tool, not a panacea. I began to learn to listen to myself, to see counselling as a creative process, rather than as a clear set of techniques that can be learnt and applied. I had to recognize and acknowledge that others did not have neat answers, even if I wished they had.

I continue to read widely; I find dialogue with other therapists and counsellors stimulating and exciting. I value enormously the contribution of others to my own development and knowledge. But I have also learnt to value and trust myself, while also attempting to monitor, question, and challenge my ideas and responses, in the same way that I do to others. I try neither to passively soak up and accept ideas simply because they are comfortable, nor to reject them because they are not. I recognize that knowledge in any field can never be absolute; rather it grows and develops with time. This is particularly so in the field of counselling. We are dealing with people not things. They cannot be put into boxes: models and theories are a useful base to our understanding, but should not become rigid and unchanging.

As time has moved on, and I do more teaching and supervision, I try to be aware of the dangers as well as the values inherent in them. They can be powerful, in the same way as counselling and therapy are for clients, although in neither instance is that always sufficiently acknowledged. This was emphasized for me following a supervision session with an inexperienced trainee counsellor.

I had commented on a particular part of the session, suggesting an alternative intervention that might have been helpful. To me, this was a suggestion and a point for discussion. It was not intended as a directive, or a pointer for her next counselling session – it was only appropriate within the context of that time. Our next supervision started with the counsellor telling me how, when she next met with her client, she had used my suggestion as soon as possible, using exactly my words. Her client had been taken aback: it was irrelevant to what she was presenting that week. The client had moved on; the counsellor remained with my words. I have learnt to be far more careful, especially with inexperienced counsellors, to encourage them to listen to themselves and their clients, as well as to me, in utilizing supervision. I hope that I am sometimes able to offer useful insights and perspectives, but I do not have answers, although as with my own recent experience, supervisees may wish I had.

Don't let the buggers get you down

The popular image of counselling and counsellors may be of sympathetic, caring people, concerned for the well-being of others. They are likely to be seen in the context of a world whose primary concern is the sharing of knowledge and ideas, the maintenance of profession standards, and in which the care and concern for clients would extend to colleagues. Another popular assumption is that counselling is a highly individualized occupation; that the consulting-room door is a barrier to political and social issues, and that they can appropriately and conveniently be left outside.

While there are many caring and generous people in this field, the picture is inevitably more diverse. Professional jealousies do exist, and can sometimes loom large. New ideas, for instance, challenges to existing training structures, can result in sharp stabs in the back, blatant dishonesty, and collusion with, and between, other powerful professional groups. There can be enormous resistance to change from those who are trained to know all about it, but do not necessarily recognize it in themselves. It is not simply a nice, friendly, little world, and it is a shock to discover that some of those who could hopefully encourage and stimulate changes and developments resist these and actively interrupt their progress.

One lesson I have learnt is not to give up. It is important, while acknowledging, examining and incorporating genuine challenge, to maintain your own integrity and hold true to your own ideas – especially when these arise from considerable and varied clinical experience. Additionally, it helps to build up your own support network of those who think similarly, though taking care not to repeat the very exclusivity you are trying to avoid, and may be reacting against.

It would be comfortable if the outside world would really not impinge on the therapeutic work. It does – and in ways that cannot be ignored. In my own working life this has occurred differently at different times. On one occasion my colleague and myself became embroiled in a dispute with our employing institution, and found our own professional integrity placed firmly on the line. Did we protect our jobs by agreeing to new conditions of service that would not guarantee confidentiality, and would also place professional decisions in the hands of an administrator? Or did we risk our jobs, but fight to maintain these most basic and essential conditions of counselling? We took the latter course and lost our jobs. I was lucky and found another immediately; my colleague did not. Perhaps the hardest thing to accept was another counsellor knowingly accepting the job on the conditions we had fought against accepting. It was also hard that so many counsellors we asked for support did not give it – apparently they did not wish to become involved in the internal politics of another institution. We had little choice. Some did fight and argue on our behalf – although unsuccessfully, but it made us feel less isolated and alone in our struggle – and nowadays professional counselling organizations have more power than then. Perhaps it would be very different today. I hope so.

On a different level, an example from clinical practice in which the outside world dramatically and unpleasantly intervened, comes to mind. A young woman presented the day after a violent sexual assault. She was scared to go to the police; she feared that their response could also be abusive. At the same time she was worried that if attacks were not reported, the attackers would not be caught. It was also clear that the likelihood of her assault could have been reduced had the area been properly lit and buildings secured. She was very distressed and physically injured. Many issues were evident: the primary one of how to best care for her being linked to others. I, too, had anxieties about police response, but could I, and should I, intervene to do some rapid 'education'? How far should I become involved in external issues and the wider implications? I did become involved in many ways, and worked with her for some time. Every step of every intervention I made was with the consent of my client, but it far exceeded what are the normal boundaries of the counselling role.

The police were receptive, and her attacker was arrested. Ultimately, both the lighting in the area and building security was improved. All these things helped to empower and heal this client in a way that I believe could not have happened had I responded in a more restricted way. The interaction between an inner self and external worlds is a complex one, but in a situation like this external realities harshly and viciously invade and cannot be ignored. And so, the lesson has two components: don't let the buggers get you down – the counselling world is a mixture of people too – and don't forget that other worlds do exist. You ignore them at your client's peril.

Conclusion

Although these five 'lessons' are in many ways very distinct, there are some features that connect them. One is the need to take care of yourself, both for your own sake and for the sake of effective practice. The importance of listening to others, but also listening to yourself, is another common thread, as is the need for boundaries, but the necessity of flexibility and sometimes (carefully) moving beyond them. To me, an important commonality, although it operates differently in the various examples, is acknowledging the existence, influence, and power of wider worlds, external pressures, and political structures. By necessity these examples have been short; more detail would have illustrated the latter point more fully. In thinking and writing about these situations I am made aware once more of the complexity of counselling. There are so many layers and levels; so many factors that influence the process. Finally, I would want just to stress the need to acknowledge these complexities, and also to look after yourself.

Index